MURPHY'S LAWS
of
SONGWRITING

WRITTEN BY

RALPH MURPHY

Murphy's Laws of Songwriting
The Book
by Ralph Murphy
Copyright © 2011/2012/2013 by Ralph Murphy.
Published by Murphy Music Consulting, Inc.
Manufactured in the United States of America.
All rights reserved.

ISBN 978-0-615-41659-5

Cover and page layout by Lynn Snyder
for Nosy Rosy Designs.
Front cover design by Kerry Murphy.

*This book is dedicated
to all those who fight for the rights
of songwriters and publishers
to earn a living doing
what they love doing.*

"Ralph Murphy's Laws are a new songwriter's tough truths, and a master class for one who has been a 'stand alone writer' for a long, long time (and finds the truths just as tough as they ever were!) Ralph has taught countless grateful students (myself included) and still loves the art and the craft and the process, and now he has taken the time to write it down ... lucky us!"

—DON SCHLITZ,
GRAMMY AWARD-WINNING SONGWITER
NASHVILLE SONGWRITER'S HALL OF FAME
NORTH CAROLINA MUSIC & ENTERTAINMENT HALL OF FAME

"I've known Ralph Murphy forever and his knowledge on the passion, heart and soul of songwriting has been an inspiration to me. Then when I started to hear him talk about his research and the ananlitical stance on the craft, science, formula and commercial viability of each song, I began telling him to write it down ... do a book ... called it 'Murphy's Laws' or something cool like that. I wasn't the only one asking him to do that either ... Almost everyone who sat through one of his talks and frantically tried to write his words of wisdom down asked for the same. Finally it is done. This is the bible for everyone from beginners to seasoned writers. Read it, learn it and BURN it so no one else will learn the secrets! Seriously, get yourself one and pass on the news to all your fellow songwriters. Thank you Ralph."

—RANDY BACHMAN
THE GUESS WHO
BACHMAN TURNER OVERDRIVE

"As a professional songwriter for over 40 years, I have met many 'experts' eager to share their opinions and tips on 'how to do it.' Ralph Murphy has done the research, written the hits, and can communicate the kind of valuable information that can actually help writers succeed in this crazy business – it's all in this book!"

—PAT ALGER
NSAI SONGWRITER OF THE YEAR, 1991
ASCAP SONGWRITER OF THE YEAR, 1992
NASHVILLE SONGWRITER'S HALL OF FAME

"Ralph Murphy knows his stuff. He is one of the few advisers that even professional songwriters turn to. There are no shortcuts to success and Ralph lays out the path to success for songwriters clearly and thoughtfully. If you are serious about the songwriting craft, then this is a MUST READ!"

—BART HERBISON, Executive Director
Nashville Songwriters Association
California Songwriters Association
Texas Songwriters Association

"*Murphy's Laws of Songwriting* is the kind of book I wish I'd had access to when I began writing songs back in the '60s. Anyone who is serious about a career in the business and craft of songwriting should have a copy of this essential book in his or her kit."

—ROGER GREENAWAY, OBE
Ivor Novello Award Winner
Songwriter's Hall of Fame

"You are holding an amazing collection of tools on how to reach your audience. If there was a hit songwriter's secret handshake, Da Murphy would probably have included it. Ralph Murphy has devoted decades to the study of 'song communication.' What makes a hit? All the ingredients are here. Simply add authenticity and your own unique voice, and maybe … just maybe … you'll join a very small club of hit songwriters. I hope so. The book is wonderful. Great stuff!"

—PAUL WILLIAMS
Oscar, Grammy and Golden Globe
Award-Winning Songwriter
Songwriter's Hall of Fame

"Nobody has more information on what makes hits, and a better way of explaining it."

—ROGER COOK
Nashville Songwriter's Hall of Fame
New York Songwriter's Hall of Fame
Ivor Novello Award Winner

"If you've been seeking the Holy Grail of Songwriting, look no further. It's in your hand! If the Songwriters Hall of Fame could condense the wisdom of all their members into one book, this would be it!"

—MICHAEL LASKOW
FOUNDER & CEO
TAXI, INDEPENDENT A&R

About the Author

RALPH MURPHY, songwriter, has been successful for five decades. Consistently charting songs in an ever-changing musical environment makes him a member of that very small group of professionals who make a living doing what they love to do. Add to that the platinum records as a producer, the widely acclaimed Murphy's Laws of Songwriting articles used as part of the curriculum at colleges, universities, and by songwriter organizations, his success as the publisher, head of, and co-owner of, the extremely successful Picalic Group of Companies, and you see a pattern of achievement based on more than luck.

Passion-driven, with a desire to know how, what, when where, and who, he is a formidable insider force. He is in worldwide demand as a lecturer on songwriting and has been a guest speaker at universities, at colleges, and for professional songwriter organizations around the globe. Murphy has served as president of the Nashville Chapter of the Recording Academy, has been a NARAS

National Trustee, and served as President of the Nashville Songwriters Association International.

In addition to serving as Vice President for the International and Domestic Membership Group of the American Society of Composers, Authors and Publishers (ASCAP), he has also served on the Southern Regional Writers Advisory Board of ASCAP, the Songwriters Guild of America regional advisory board, and is a member of NSAI, NARAS, CMA, CCMA, SAC, SGA, and ASCAP. In 2012, Ralph was inducted into the Canadian Country Music Hall of Fame.

TABLE OF CONTENTS

INTRODUCTION

A LOT OF PEOPLE make the assumption that once they cross the line from amateur to professional in whatever their chosen field may be, that there is nothing more for them to learn. They just go about performing their role based on skills they have already acquired, but learning should never stop.

Just read the back flap of any major novel to see how grateful the writer is to his or her editor. Just watch the post-game show from any major golf tournament, and you will hear the winner compliment the pro who changed his swing, his putting or his chipping.

Well, just like any other pro, my role is to tweak a songwriter's approach to his or her craft so that they can produce songs personalized with their own stamp that will resonate with the marketplace.

Unfortunately, most writers only see their songs from the inside out. Fortunately for them, I am seeing their songs from the outside in. Once I start pointing out the weaknesses in their work, they invariably see them and respond by making the work more accessible to the listener.

Strangely enough, this is a function I can't perform for myself. I have to seek out my own pros. I'm deeply grateful to them all.

This book represents a voyage of discovery. As a child, watching the joy/solace/comfort/pure pleasure people took in singing songs, I wanted to be the creator/provider of those songs. I wanted to write the words and music that became "their song." I wanted to hear those songs sung in clubs, on the street, in the car, and in grocery stores. I wanted people dancing, falling in love, falling out of love, skating, or doing dishes to them. In other words, I wanted "hits." Not just hits but big hits … hits that would last.

Riding a wave of rare good fortune, my search – early on – led me to great and patient older "hit" writers who were willing to share the insights of their professional voyage of discovery with the insanely dysfunctional teen writer that I was. I am forever thankful to them.

This book is the result of absorbing all the craft and insight given, applying it over time, successfully to multiple genres, and observing patterns that fulfill listener expectations when applied to those genres. In other words, consumers of music want what they want, like what they like and, as the creators of that music, "we" are writing for "them." In these pages are keys to doors. As you unlock them and walk through, remember, write smart, but write with your heart, and pitch smarter.

You are entering the "Music Business."

Welcome home!

CHAPTER 1

WHAT BROUGHT ME TO THE DANCE

Uncle Art: "Think Like the Fish"

MY UNCLE ART HAD A PASSION FOR FISHING.

He knew how fast the fish that he wanted to catch swam; what it ate at any given time of day, month or year; when it mated and where it did it, and if candles and wine were involved. He knew every idiosyncratic detail about the fish themselves and understood millions of other tiny factors (current, wind, etc.) that make catching fish a crap shoot for most people who set out to put fish on the table. He would eye the gadget-filled boat palaces trolling up and down the river and smile.

Using the fish-filled cooler as a foot rest, he would lean forward, put his hand on his knee, get his face on the same level as mine, and tell me for the three-thousandth time (making the three-thousandth telling as intense as the first), "when you go fishing … you don't think like a fisherman … you think like the fish!"

He was as proud of this pearl of wisdom as I was baffled by its meaning. It wasn't until many years later, in a completely different context, that I began to understand. But before I get to all of that, here's the condensed version of my story.

Songs Open Doors

There always seemed to be a piano around back then, and my mother played it and knew all the popular songs of the day. That made her popular, too!

The songs that she played were door-openers to instant approval from everyone. She (and I by association) was eagerly accepted because of the music she played and the songs that we would all sing as she played. As a kid that was an amazing revelation to me. Having watched my mother's ability to open doors with a song, I tried to play piano as well. It just wasn't my instrument.

Fast-forward a little bit. When I was about 11 years old, my mother bought me a guitar out of a mail order catalog. It came with a chord book and an extra set of strings. I quickly learned two chords and went out looking for songs that had two chords. I couldn't find any so I wrote one and played it for some friends. They were impressed and asked whose song it was. When I told them that I had written it, I suddenly gave me cache. I, a scrawny kid, was instantly cool.

A growth spurt when I was about twelve made me more or less the same height as I am today; so by the time I was thirteen or fourteen, I was, outwardly, adult-looking. I learned a couple more chords, and I was ready to reach for the stars. With the encouragement of the wonderfully talented musician/writer/arranger Barbara Thornton, I played around my home town in Ontario, Canada, in different groups with other musicians. I became pretty well-known locally.

Finding the Song - One Place at a Time

At about the same time, there was a healthy music scene in Los Angeles that seemed to call. Folk was the "genre du jour" back then. How convenient that that music was the bulk of the repertoire played by the duo that Jack Klaeysen and I had formed. So, a move to LA seemed like a logical decision for us. Getting there was a problem. Suddenly a window opened! Dave Thomas, a family friend, was transferring to LA with his family and wanted his car out there. He needed someone to share the driving. So, Jack and I loaded our guitars in Dave's car, a brand new white Pontiac convertible, connected to Route 66 in Chicago, and drove Route 66 all the way to LA.

In Los Angeles there were (it seemed) a million songwriters, all looking to get their songs cut, just like we were. I tried to write songs that people would love and adore. They seemed to like them, but we couldn't get anywhere business-wise.

On my own, I tried New York. I went and looked at the Brill Building, walked through the halls, heard people singing their songs, heard them pounding through the opaque glass that seemed to pass for walls between the offices and the hallway. I went to Jack Dempsey's restaurant downstairs and saw Jack Dempsey greeting all the music business "big dogs" as they came in, but I was still excluded. I returned to Canada.

Then in 1963 I heard the Beatles and I knew where I had to be ... Liverpool. I also needed to raise the money to get there. I heard about an opportunity as a ship's cook (I couldn't cook) on an ocean-going dredge that was dredging the Great Lakes to cut the path for the St. Lawrence Seaway. The problem was that you had to be both a cook *and* 19 years

old to join the Seaman's Union. I was neither, so I
lied. I got my union card *and* the job and worked
16 hours a day, 7 days a week, for a few months. I
made enough money to buy a boat ticket, and after
that, over the next 18 months, Jack and I gigged
constantly and saved enough to pay for our travel. In
February of '65 we went back to New York, caught
the boat and headed for Liverpool.

After a short stint in Liverpool, we realized that the
music "business" was in London, so a few months
later we moved to London. We got signed to a
record deal with Pye Records. Tony Hatch, who was
a very hot writer/producer at the time with Petula
Clark, (he wrote *Downtown, Don't Sleep in the
Subway*, etc.), was producing us.

Well, we were playing clubs, and in the clubs they
loved us. We were the darlings of the Kings Road,
a very fashionable area in West London where the
"trendy" people hung out in the '60s.

Lesson #1 - The Song Has to Stand On its Own

Quick break here from my story for a retrospective
look at my first lesson learned:

In clubs there are a few reasons why the audience loves you, and you think it's all about your songs. The top five reasons in order of importance to the audience are:

1. Wow, you've got a great personality!

2. Man, you sang the heck out of that song! Gosh you're good.

3. I love this club. I'm so glad we came here tonight.

4. Wow, the wine list is really cool, the beer is cold and the bar snacks are excellent!

5. Man, I like those songs.

Well, the place and time you most want your songs to be heard and appreciated is at drive time (the period of time most commuters are stuck in their cars with nothing to do but listen to the radio), and that is a situation where your song has to work extra hard to be liked.

Your songs are orphans. They have to stand all by themselves. They don't have the benefit of being associated with a great wine list or an awesome club, or your winning personality. Selling a recording which is separated from the live experience is a completely different proposition. You are approaching people in a situation where they are not necessarily predisposed to give a new song a shot. They want familiarity, and your new song doesn't offer that familiarity.

Successful Club Songs Don't Mean Cutable Hits

Jack and I didn't know that then. If we had, it certainly would have made things a little easier for us. So, you get to learn from our early lessons.

Anyway, the day after a successful gig at a club, I would go into the record company and play them those same songs that had won approval from the audience the night before. The powers-that-be at the label would simply say, "They don't work." Looking back, I realize that what they meant was that the songs didn't work for the different area of the music industry that they were targeting … where people were not necessarily going to give our songs the benefit of the doubt. The songs were duds outside of the clubs.

So I had to rethink and relearn, and at the time, thankfully for me, there were a lot of really great writers around London who were willing to share their knowledge. If I start naming some of them, I'd have to name them all. They were really wonderful people, excellent writers and great mentors. (And I am trying to keep this book short!)

Lesson #2 - The Song Has to be Better than Anyone Else's

But it never occurred to me then that what they really were was stand-alone writers. What I mean by a stand-alone writer is a writer who is not part of the production company, the artist's team or the record label. Those writers perform their role independent of, and outside of, the "inner circle." The songs they write have to be much better than the ones the artist, producer or anyone connected to project has been able to create or they won't be recorded and will never become a hit.

Those songs have to be good on multiple levels. They must resonate with the audience. They must enable the artist to look good to their fans. They also have to be accessible enough for the "average listener" to relate to without being so ordinary that they don't stand out from other songs. Lastly, they must possess all the features I will address in this book.

I Get My First Hit – Thanks to Mentors

Because of those wonderful stand-alone writers who were willing to work with me in all the weak areas of my writing, I had my first stand-alone hit in 1966, *Call My Name,* by James Royal. This was the first taste I had of someone else cutting one of my songs outside of an act that I was part of, and I liked it! Although I was still recording and touring, outside cuts followed by the Casuals, Vanity Fair, the High Windows, etc.

Later on, in 1969, after I stopped touring, I moved to New York as a producer/writer. I saw the same basic song structures and forms. They were exactly the same, but I was entering the world of Rock and Dance music, as opposed to Pop. Thankfully, the only aspects that seemed to change from genre to genre were the vocabulary and the technology, sounds, instruments and production values.

Nashville - By Happy Accident

Well, just as one of the Rock acts that I was producing, April Wine, went gold, I accidentally had a Country hit in 1971 with Jeannie C. Riley, singing a song I had written called, *Good Enough To Be Your Wife.* An artist named Janet Lawson on United Artists had released the song as a Pop single, and then that recording wound up in the hands of an A&R guy down in Nashville. He thought it would be good for Jeannie C. Riley, and the next thing I knew, I got a call from the producer, Shelby Singleton at Plantation Records, telling me that the song was #2 on the Country chart.

I went down to Nashville to collect my ASCAP award for *Good Enough to be Your Wife* and fell in love with the place. By immersing myself in the genre. I soon discovered that all the same rules of songwriting that I'd been using for Pop songs applied to Country songs. But, of course, the technology, instrumentation, and definitely the vocabulary were different.

The Birth of My Analysis Methods

Later on in the 70s when I moved to Nashville, I started Picalic Music, a publishing company, with Roger Cook, who has co-writes on *Long Cool Woman In A Black Dress* by the Hollies, *Teach the World to Sing* by the New Seekers, and many more. He has since been inducted in to the Nashville Songwriters Association Hall Of Fame as well as the New York Songwriters Hall of fame. Roger was also the co-writer on our first Picalic hit, *Talking in Your Sleep*, by Crystal Gayle.

Picalic was a weird sort of evolutionary process for me. When Roger and I talked about starting a publishing company, it was going to be very organic and very small. Neither Roger nor I wanted a corporation. He wanted to get out of London, and I really wanted to get out of New York, since it was getting harder to raise kids in the city. We talked about Los Angeles. We had both worked out there a lot, but neither of us really wanted to move out there.

Because I'd had a Country hit down in Nashville and Roger had already fallen in love with the city, we decided to make a go of a publishing company in Nashville. He'd met a couple of other writers that he was very impressed with while he was down there: Bobby Wood with whom Roger co-wrote *Talking in Your Sleep* for Crystal Gayle, and with whom I co-wrote *Half the Way* for Crystal. Bobby and I teamed up again to write *He Got You* for Ronnie Milsap. All of those songs were #1 hits. As long as the story was original and engaging, we were winners.

Because I really didn't understand the commercial aspects of the genre, I would gather all the number one Country Billboard records and analyze them. I would check them for:

- seconds to first use of title
- number of repetitions of title
- vocabulary
- which song structures they primarily used.

I began to see a pattern. As that pattern was revealed through my analysis, I learned that if I pitched songs that had the same kind of template as existing #1 songs, Roger and I as a publishing company, our writers, and ourselves could have #1s as well I had a basic grounding in publishing from having been director of production for Belwin-Mills Publishing in New York for seven years. That company had a large print division, so I got a perspective on that area of the business. I also worked closely with the people who did the nuts and bolts of licensing. We issued a lot of "synch" licenses (film and TV) and also worked extensively in musical theater with shows like "Pippin" and "The Magic Show." So, aside from writing and producing, I brought to Picalic a view of the industry from a business level.

NOTES:

CHAPTER 2

YOUR SONGS - MAKE THEM WORK FOR YOU *AND* PAY YOU

The Publisher/Writer Relationship and Roles

AS I ASSUMED MORE and more of the business role at Picalic, I had to look at signing writers. That meant that I had to be able to assess them based on a whole list of criteria, starting with their creative ability, all the way to appropriate uses for their works and the value of them. A publisher is outside the creative equation, i.e., not the writer of the song, so the publisher will have a different perspective on the song.

Everything that I was studying about what was happening at radio with the sound of the records, e.g., the structure of the songs and the vocabulary that was being used, I applied to the work coming from any new young writer that was coming in.

Breaking In - Gradually

As a new writer, you approach a publisher over a period time, sometimes six to nine months, even up to a year, and play the publisher the songs until they are convinced that you have the work ethic, the creativity, and that you also have the expertise from a craft perspective. Craft is a major consideration.

Something else that is of primary importance to the publisher is that you have a good personality, because you have to develop social skills! You have to go out and meet artists and producers. You must bring a lot more to the table than simply the ability to write songs.

You have to be able to write great songs and then know enough about the business to go out and do something with them. The writers I worked with stayed current with everything that was going on with the industry, and brought me suggestions about where we should be pitching their songs.

What's your contribution?

So, after I determined that I wanted to do a deal with a writer, they would create what we refer to as a "Schedule A." The Schedule A is what the writer brings with him/her to any publishing deal. It can be 8, 10, 20 or more songs that they've written, in whole or in part, that are going to be part of the publishing situation ongoing.

As a publisher, what I wanted was to have at least two or three songs in the Schedule that I thought had the potential to be hits, so that when the deal was signed, I could be out on the street pitching songs within 24 hours of signing that writer.

How Is It Working Today

In today's market, that is even more important because most publishers work for corporations. When they sign you, they can't wait a year or 18 months for you to get something going …they have to hit the road running. If, in three years' time, it's all red ink that's being reported back to their corporate bosses (many of whom are working in other divisions of a conglomerate, and who may even be part of a foreign company that owns that publisher), there's going to be trouble. Red ink = bad. Black ink = good! Black ink is what the owners of today's music publishing company are really interested in. They need to keep that black ink flowing back to their shareholders. By the way, the conventional wisdom among publishers is that, if they say "no" to signing writers 100 percent of the time, they will be right 95 percent of the time. Don't give them any reason to say "no," and your songs will be the reason they say "yes."

Know Your Market (Your Fish!)

Who is it for you? Couples dancing at midnight? Teens? Women driving to work? Pick one, they will be your fish. That is what writing hits is all about. I will repeat that message to you about the same number of times my Uncle Art reminded me. That's what this book is about.

Be More Than an "Anyone" - Be a Professional

But... you say, "anyone" can go fishing. Well, the same way "anyone" can go fishing, and "anyone" can play golf, and "anyone" can play tennis, "anyone" can write a song. But ... the chasm between the casual "anyones" who do all of the above, and the successful professionals at the top of their game is huge. The professional songwriters, whose work earns them a very comfortable living year in and year out for their entire lives plus (in the United States) 70 years after their death, are as unique as professional athletes.

The parallels between the professional athlete and the professional songwriter are startling. Self-awareness (a working knowledge of personal strengths, weaknesses, and a passion to grow and change), and craft/technique internalized and engaged, so totally that the result can be called art. I've been told that Ernest Hemingway would sit down every day and write a hundred words – drunk or sober. He knew you have to keep the machinery functioning. Keep going. Write the bad to find the good. The skills needed by the professional writer are honed by use.

Writers tell me all the time that they have written hundreds of songs and none have been successful yet. I tell them that they are just writing through the ordinary songs to get to the good songs that will lead them to the great ooooh factor, (i.e., when you play the song and listeners go "ooooh," can you play that again?).

There are, however, additional hurdles for the would-be professional songwriter. In this book, I am either talking to you or to some songwriter you are trying to help, so it's time to get personal. If you want to make money doing what you love/need/must/are driven/have to do…

This book is not about teaching you how to write songs … you're already doing that … you have to.

Lose the Whine, the Bitterness, the Sermon

Watching writers battle through their cathartic self-congratulatory, self-loathing, fragmented, partially told stories set to music is not pretty or pleasant.

Typically, when writers discover that they have this wonderful gift, the three things they feel that they have a mandate to do are whine, preach and vent. The last thing I want to hear coming out of the speaker of my clock radio at 7am is someone whining, preaching and venting unless it is done with lots of humor, irony and detail.

Bitterness and preaching do not result in songs that millions of people hum, sing, whistle, buy, download, steal, turn their friends on to, what they make love to, smile to, cry to, and that ultimately pop up in TV shows, movies and those annoying, but lucrative, commercials. Those are not the songs that people will love for the rest of their lives, and for decades after the writer has shuffled off these earthly charts, and are writing for that great publisher in the stars. The works you create will remain behind to be part of the lives of future generations.

Connection, it's all about connection

So, understand that some of your songs are great for your personal catharsis, but they are simply bad for business. Remember, a random listener hearing your work for the first time does not care about you like your family and friends do. However, if you do your job effectively, you might make a connection with that listener in three-and-a-half minutes that will last forever. And think how excited your family and friends will be when you start writing hits!

Find the money!

And by the way, as a happy by-product, your family will be very well taken care of. If you'd like to know how lucrative a successful songwriter can be, check out the following:

I have asked permission from Todd and Jeff Brabec, authors of the essential music industry handbook Music Money and Success: the Insiders Guide to Making Money in the Music Business, to reprint some information from their book. This demonstrates how much you can potentially earn from your compositions.

The chart below shows many of the areas that you can earn money from, if you write a hit song with crossover and international success. It has to be the right type of song to get involved with all the opportunities mentioned but it is possible.

- $9,100 U.S. single sales (100,000 copies)
- $45,500 U.S. album sales (500,000 copies)
- $600,000 U.S. radio and TV performances
- $11,000 Foreign single sales
- $67,000 Foreign album sales
- $900,000 Foreign radio and TV performances
- $25,000 Print
- $175,000 Commercial
- $19,000 Television series use and video
- $40,000 Motion picture use
- $4,000 Foreign theatrical performances of Film
- $142,000 Broadway show
- $15,000 Video games
- $14,000 Ringtones
- $1,200 Lyric reprint in a novel
- $40,000 Toys, cards, and dolls
- $3,000 Karaoke
- $2,000 Live Concerts
- $35,000 Internet
- $2,147,800 Total Writer / Publisher Income

For example, if the song has 100,000 individual track downloads and is on a 500,000-unit selling album, the total mechanical royalties will be $54,600, if the song is licensed at the 9.1 cent statutory rate in the United States.

If it becomes a major radio hit, the writer and publisher performance royalties can easily earn $600,000.

If the song is used as background in a scene on *CSI* or *Grey's Anatomy,* another $19,000 in television and home video fees can be generated.

The song might be used as part of a scene in a major motion picture for a fee of $40,000.

When that film is shown in theatres outside the United States, foreign performance rights societies will collect additional performance royalties from the theatres ($4,000 in the example).

The song might be put into a hit catalogue/jukebox musical on Broadway and earn its pro-rated share of 3 to 4 percent of the weekly box office receipts.
It might be licensed to a music-based videogame for $15,000 (the royalties for one song based on a million units).

The song might be used as a ringtone at 24 cents per download to mobile phones. Ringbacks are also licensed.

Because the song has a strong melody and message, it might be licensed for use in musical greeting cards, e-cards and also as the song in a singing toy.

A karaoke game company licenses the song and lyrics for an online site.

The song is also performed by the recording artist on a successful concert tour; again generating performance royalties for the writer and publisher.

A print company issues sheet music, an album folio, and "how to play" versions of the song and record.

A major car company chooses the song to be used in its national television, internet and radio campaign to introduce a new model.

Various internet sites stream the song and use it in their programming.

And the song receives radio airplay and record sales/downloads in countries outside the United States, not only because of the popularity of the artist, but also from the local language versions recorded in various countries because of its strong melody.

NOTES:

CHAPTER 3

THE SONGWRITER'S JOB

Your Job (As *YOU* See It)

SO LET'S GO BACK to the gifts you were given at birth: that disproportionate depth of perception coupled with an overwhelming need to communicate your insight. These gifts have been forged by life experiences, and, more than likely, many of those experiences were painful ones. It would appear that your depth of dysfunction, and your desire to share your experiences, would combine to make you the perfect messenger. Your ability to whine, preach and vent is exceptional.

Orphans and products of monumentally dysfunctional families, some of which have been scarred by murders or suicides, appear to be particularly good candidates for songwriter of the year! Then, factor in physical, sexual or emotional abuse, and we begin to get a picture of the motivations for many songwriters.

So, if you have an acute inability to communicate on a personal level, are bad at relationships, yet have an overpoweringly desperate, desperate, desperate desire to be loved, you might be on your way to the Hall of Fame! (Not really!)

Lucky you!

Again, the only problem you have is … no one cares! (Really!)

Your Job (What It *REALLY* Is)

Let's get back to when you were a consumer rather than a provider of songs.

The writers of your favorite songs gave you "You." Yes, I just said this a few pages ago, but I'm going to say it again, just as Uncle Art did with me.

The writers of those favorite songs gave you "You" successfully because of two things:

- · 1 The first was mastery of their craft.
- · 2 The second was the ability to get their whining, preaching, venting, dysfunctional selves out of the way in order to let their insightful and well-forged creativity shine through.

When craft and creativity collide, the result is wonderful! And that's the path you have chosen. Making money from your craft/creativity is important for a variety of reasons. However, the two reasons that are miles ahead of the rest are physical survival (eating is good), and validation (you are worthy, they like you)!

Anyone who's been rich and then poor will tell you that rich was better. Also, when you write songs that others love, and you get paid for it, you feel validated. Your songs, and, by association, you, are worth something! They like you, they really like you! You are worthy, and you can pay your bills … what a concept!

To a certain extent I'm exaggerating here, but song-writers are a uniquely strange crew. Aren't we?

Know Your Own Strengths

One of the top ten questions I get asked by newcomers to the industry is, "How do I get heard in the music business?" Before I can answer that, I have to know exactly what they want to be "heard." When I ask them about their goals – whether they want to be songwriters or recording artists – the most common response is, "Both."

Listen to the Truth

The unfortunate truth of the matter is that, while many of the newcomers I counsel may be gifted as songwriters or as singers, very, very few are equally blessed with both talents. While one ability may come rather naturally, the other often needs significant honing.

The problem is, not everyone wants to hear the truth. Some great singers (who are average songwriters) can make the really average songs they've written shine through the sheer power of their vocal ability. They make the phrase "I love you" sound so good that you almost believe they invented it. In equal numbers come the great songwriters (who are average singers) who have been told by family, friends, lovers, and late-night adoring coffeehouse/honkytonk buffoons that, despite the fact that their tempo, pitch and teeth are bad, they have star quality. And no matter how badly they sing, their songs are still strong enough to survive a mediocre vocal performance and sound like hits. (This is the only reason karaoke manufacturers are not hunted for sport!)

Check Your Ego at the Door

The bottom line is: lose your ego. It's called "absenting of self." The person most likely to come between you and your career goal is you. Don't make the best of your talent a donkey for the least of your talent. Get some unbiased feedback from industry pros (available through a variety of NSAI programs), and if you are indeed weaker in one area, focus on your strength.

If you're a great singer – but an average writer – don't be upset if someone loves your voice but wants you to sing someone else's songs. Go find those great songs while you learn to become a better writer. By the same token, if you're a great songwriter – but an average singer – don't be upset if someone wants to record your songs but passes on you as an artist. Remember, this is called the music "business," and the business end of our industry knows that the majority of the G.A.P. (Great American Public) just wants to hear great records. They don't lie awake nights wondering who wrote and/or sang the songs they like on the radio.

Be Smart

If you have a sneaking suspicion that the preceding law even remotely applies to you, then do yourself this favor: picture the music industry as a large building with an entrance for singers on one side, and an entrance for songwriters on the other. Maybe you can't go through both doors at the same time, but you can concentrate on getting inside through the door that opens the most easily for you. Who knows? Once you're inside, you can end up just about anywhere.

NOTES:

CHAPTER 4

KNOW YOUR AUDIENCE

Match the Song and the Beat to the Use

THERE ARE A LOT OF FACTORS that impact how musical uses are valued. Couples dancing at midnight want slamming 120 to 140 beats per minute (BPM) rhythm, identifiable melodic hooks, memorable choruses that might have a call and response segment to them, and probably an extended remix of the song for maximum time on the dance floor.

A commuter at drive-time wants a couple of upbeat familiar songs to get them in a good mood before they lock themselves up in their office for the day. An audience in a folk club doesn't flinch at seven or eight choruses and verses because, at some point, they'll all be able to join in and sing along. All those uses of music are consistent with audience expectations.

Be Honest, Don't Kid Yourself

Hymns at a polka festival or polkas at a funeral would be as much a part of the audience expectation as heavy metal at an intimate candle-lit dinner.

In any genre, you, as a creator, must think like your audience. You must think like the kind of fish you are trying to catch.

Drive-Time is a Gold Mine

No matter what you've been told about the internet, the most captive listener is the "drive-time" working stiff. The maximum exposure that you can get for your record/song currently is drive-time. This, according to market research, is when the audience is concentrated and captive … also incredibly distracted. When I'm writing, to give myself the hardest possible target, I imagine a person in a relationship with someone they're not crazy about, having dressed and fed their kids, now dropping them at day care. They are driving to a job they hate, having to work for a boss who's a jerk, in a car that's about to break down in the rain.

That's the "fish" you're after. If your song captures them, it can engage anyone.

What's the difference between charming a family member who's sitting on the living room couch and eager to hear your latest song, or holding the attention a few million harried humans at drive-time? It is the difference between frying an egg and cooking a 10-course dinner for 200 gourmands. The latter is the job of the stand-alone writer. See more about the stand-alone writer in the next chapter.

The 7:00 AM Rule

If you're ready to stop being "warm and fuzzy," go for the throat and write a hit – read on, you're ready for "The 7:00 a.m. Rule." Everybody already thinks you're crazy anyway, so you might as well be successful and crazy. It will make your mother and your bank manager happy.

Think about what you want to do at 7:00 a.m. The real answer: nothing. Your car isn't running right, your kids are driving you crazy, your boss is on your back, you burned your hand on the toaster, and all the while, under a half-dead plant, a collection of transistors and plastic called a radio is relentlessly trying to capture your attention.

The Road Test

Contrary to popular opinion, songs are not really "sold" in an A&R person's office at 11:00 a.m., a publisher's office at 2:00 p.m., a manager's office at 4:00 p.m., or a coffeehouse, bar, concert or nightclub at 10:00 p.m. After all the work of the creative process - the politics of pitching, the hell of being on hold, the anguish of the recording process, the torment of waiting to be the single - comes the acid test. It's called "Drive Time."

There are two drive times - morning and afternoon. The one I chose for my target audience is the toughest ... morning. My target "drive time" occurs between 6:30 a.m. and 8:30 a.m. on radio stations around the world. It can take the song that your publisher said was a smash, the A&R people said couldn't miss, the artist hailed as a career maker, and your significant other wept over, and make it just another stain on the great toilet roll of life.

Be the "Fish"

In order to understand what will happen to your work when it is fed to the listener, it's essential to think like the listener. When you go fishing, think like the fish. A fish does not bite on a hook because it thinks it is a stainless steel hook; the fish has got to believe it has found lunch. If the bait, for any reason, does not behave like lunch, the fish goes looking elsewhere, and so does the listener.

There's No Substitution for Craft

Remember, songwriters, the listener doesn't care about you: they care about themselves as you see them. The reason you fell in love with songs before you became caught up in the mechanics of writing was because you identified with the song. You didn't care if the writer was having a good day or a bad day.

Also, the listener is used to receiving information in a certain form. There are definite song structures. The ways that a story is delivered have been in place longer than any of us have been alive: starting with a killer opening line; having a beginning, middle and end; changing rhyme schemes from verse to chorus; choosing the right pronouns; placing the right metaphor. These and other basic elements of craft are the essential tools of the "hit" writer.

Remember, you are born with the gift of perception, but craft is an acquired skill. At 7:00 a.m., the listener is taking no prisoners. You're going to need all the craft that every other hit writer is bringing to bear.

Your Music Enhances Experiences

Remember, the only time you will hear your song played in public is if someone is making money from it. No business would spend a nickel on anything that did not earn money for the business. Sound systems cost money. Next time you are in a restaurant and you hear jazz music, check the prices on the menu. You'll probably be paying a third more for the food.

If you are in an elevator hearing music, remember that when the Otis Corporation invented the self-locking elevator in the 1930s, nobody would ride them because they were frightened. So many deaths had been caused by cables breaking on elevators prior to Mr. Otis' invention, that people were naturally afraid to ride.

Mr. Otis' solution?

He installed speakers in the elevators, and played calming music so that the passengers wouldn't panic when the doors closed.

Mr. Otis got rich!

Your Song Better Be *Way Better* Than Good

The opportunities for income sources for your music seem limitless: bars, restaurants, clubs, dance clubs, radio, television, movies, toys, ring tones and anywhere else that money is made. When music is used as a part of the experience, songwriters and publishers will make money.

However, as a songwriter in the music business today, your customer/listener is a rapidly moving target. They may hear your song for a few seconds while they're working out at the gym, and then hear it again while they're listening to an internet radio station, or through a podcast from some blogger they respect. Regardless of how the music gets to them, just remember that the same rules apply as for drive-time commercial radio. In fact, the rules may be even more brutal for the new music spaces that the internet has created. The competition is so fierce, and the amount of music available to the consumer at any given moment is so vast, that your songs are going to have to work harder than ever to stand out.

A major factor involved in this equation for success is that writers are paid on a percentage of what is earned by the people who use their songs to make money. The harder the music has to work to get the listener's attention, the more financially valuable the song is. Just remember back to Mr. Otis's elevator the next time you sit down to write a song, and try to imagine creating a song so soothing, yet so alluring, that it would make people risk their lives just to hear it. Or a song so engaging that the most harried human being on the planet will sing along.

NOTES:

CHAPTER 5

THE STAND ALONE WRITER

I HAVE SPENT THE BULK OF MY CAREER as a "stand alone" writer. I guess I had become my mentors. Let me remind you of what I said in the very first chapter.

Simply stated – if you are not the artist, producer or engineer signed to the producer's publishing company, or a close relative of the act, etc., you are a stand-alone writer. That means that whatever you write has to be better suited for the audience that the act is communicating with than the songs created by the artists themselves - and all the talent surrounding them.

Start with a Hit Song

Most industry professionals know that if you want a hit record, it really helps to start with a potential hit song. What's a hit song? That's a song that you believe the listening audience will identify with. It will stun you, however, that there are so many successful producers and A&R management types who wouldn't know a hit from a ham sandwich. That is why it's important for you, the writer, to understand the market and give these gate-keepers the perfect vehicle to carry their artists to the top of the charts. In every case, my fellow stand-aloner, it is necessary to think like the fish … AND the would-be fisherman.

Think about it. If you have $10,000 that you have saved up for a lifetime, and you're going off to Alaska to fish for salmon, the one person that you're going to be looking for when you arrive there is "the guide" who knows everything there is to know about salmon. They know the right bait to use, the depth where the fish swim, what time of day they eat, and where they mate. You expect that "the guide" can (for a price) put you in exactly the right spot to catch some fish and have a wonderful experience. You're not going to go hire some rank amateur who barely knows more about what you're trying to do than you yourself do.

Be the Go-To Guide

An artist and their record label can spend up to a million dollars on a project in much the same way. They're going to want to find someone (a "guide") who "thinks like the fish" i.e., who knows just what the audience that they're aiming at wants and how to connect with that audience. They might be pushing the song primarily through an MTV video or working it to drive-time radio. Regardless of what their promotional methods may be, they are going to need the right song to fit into those media in order to have a chance at a hit record. And remember, that is their goal: to sell copies of the record. That's how record labels make money: selling records either digitally or physically. Well, one way or another, they pay to get the song on radio. Aside from radio promotion, they will often pay many thousands of dollars to produce a music video and that video will rarely generate any real revenue for the record label.

So the song could be a hit and get lots of airplay on radio or rotations on MTV, and yet the record can still fail because the song didn't connect enough with the fans to make them want to acquire a copy of the recording. In the eyes of the record label that will mean that you, as the writer, have failed to do your job.

Finding *Your* "Fish" - *Your* Opportunities

There are many artists that aim for men as their listening audience. Unfortunately for you, the stand-alone writer, they mostly write their own material, or they and their management select writers and co-writers.

Likewise, singer/songwriters touring and playing for people at 10 o'clock at night don't require your skills.

Artists working in Urban, Hip-Hop, Rock and Roll, and Heavy Metal probably don't need what you create.

I'm not saying that there aren't opportunities for writers to collaborate with artists in those genres, but it's rare for a wholly-written song by an outside songwriter to make it onto one of those records.

Trust Me, the Fish are Female

So, you know who will record your song?
Here's who: male artists, female artists, and groups that sing TO women.

Then who are you writing for? WOMEN.

I write songs for men to sing to women, and for women to sing to women. It was my good fortune to be befriended many years ago at a bar in Nashville by a silver-haired writer by the name of Harlan Howard. Harlan was not only my dear friend (I called him the brother I never wanted), but every songwriter's best friend. His insights, and his willingness to share them, made him the stuff of legend.

His assertion was that women physically bought 50 percent of all hit records, and made men buy the other 50 percent. Translated: that means that men have to like it – but women have to love it. Women have to be engaged and held for three to four minutes, for weeks, months and hopefully years. Think of your retirement! All the research I have done over the years has proven him 90 percent correct.

NOTES:

CHAPTER 6

CO-WRITING

The Realities of Co-Writing

FIRST, FIGURE OUT where you're going.

When you are going to co-write with someone you have never worked with before, do your homework.

Ask them to give you a CD or link to two or three of their newer songs that they are excited about. This applies even to a hit writer, because past hits may not necessarily reflect his or her current attitude toward writing.

If the co-writer is an artist, get a copy of his or her latest recorded work. Ask them if they loved or hated it, because either way, you will have a sense of direction when you sit down to write with them.

Be prepared. You can't over-prepare.

Bring Something to Put Into the Game

Now, most important of all, bring at least two covered dishes to the picnic: if they don't like your potato salad, they may love your fried chicken. In other words, your co-writer may not be into a big ballad that day, but may really get off on a song at 120 beats per minute. If you both bring a couple of ideas to the session, odds are that out of the four ideas, one will appeal to both of you.

Don't Force It

If none of the ideas work out, go have lunch or dinner. Talk about the weather or golf or knitting or fishing (not religion or politics) and then book another time a few days down the road to try to write again. If you repeat the process, and it still doesn't work, you may be better off as good friends than frustrated co-writers.

Co-Writing with Established Songwriters

I had lunch one day with a new writer who had just been signed to his first major publishing deal. He told me that his publisher had been setting up co-writing appointments for him with established writers, and that he had some questions on how to approach writing on such a different level. Addressing his two biggest questions right here might be useful to writers in similar situations.

1. ***"Why does my publisher set me up to write with some established writers and not others?"***

A good publisher has four functions:
- administrator
- banker
- promoter, and
- nurturer.

It is while wearing his nurturer hat that the publisher may target three or four hit writers as co-writers, but he might be reluctant to follow through on his newly-signed writer's request to work with some other major writers.

It's not that the publisher isn't being thorough, or that his faith in his new writer is half-hearted. It's actually a matter of balance. A publisher signs a writer for his strengths (lyrics, music, assembly) and works to develop that writer in areas where he or she may fall a little short of the mark. Using his knowledge of the writer's community, the publisher puts the new writer together with someone whose strengths are complementary.

It's pointless, and frustrating, for two great lyricists to sit in a room together trying to find a great melody; likewise, it is equally pointless for two great melody writers to sit waiting for pearls of wisdom to drop from each other's lips. No one benefits.

2. *"Why am I almost always expected to be the one to provide the hook (title) and a large portion of the song when I co-write with established writers?"*

Bear in mind that co-writing requires an understanding of each other's approach to writing. The established writer knows almost nothing about his or her new co-writer; whereas the novice generally is very aware of the experienced writer's form (lyrical and melodic), language, and approach to the hook from radio, video, records, etc.

The only way for the established writer to find out about the new co-writer is to walk with him or her through the thought processes which got him from point A to point B.

Remember that successful collaboration doesn't mean that you necessarily have to be best friends. The only important thing is the quality of the song, and if the partnership doesn't work, don't worry. There are 800 #1 songwriters in Nashville. And at least 2,000 #1 songwriters worldwide. Keep trying, there is room for 2,801.

NOTES:

CHAPTER 7

SINGER /
SONGWRITERS

I'M SURE SOME OF YOU might be saying to yourself, "But I do want to be an artist as well as a songwriter." Allow me to speak directly to the singer/songwriter readers for a moment.

The chasm between the singer/songwriter and the stand-alone songwriter is really evident in what we've just looked at. In order to be a successful performing artist/writer, you must have a very forceful personality, you must be driven and single-minded, and you must be able to overcome initial audience indifference.

If you are convinced that you have a mission, a message, and a voice that deserves to be heard, you will achieve status.

Slightly Different Rules of the Game

As part of your voyage through your creative life, your songs will reflect your very personal journey. You are free to vent about a lost love, and, if you feel the need, what a loser you are. After taking five minutes to explain what the song is about, you can spin a preachy, whining, cautionary tale guaranteed to make someone sitting in a club or coffeehouse with a glass of wine at 10 o'clock at night weep and tell you after the show how touched they were. They might even tell you what a genius you are.

You can have 10 verses.

You can keep the same rhyme scheme verse to chorus.

You don't even need a chorus!

But, Do You Resonate with the Listeners?

However, when those same audience members are driving to work the next morning, listening to the radio and thinking about how to get through their day in one piece, and also thinking about where they are going to spend their disposable income (think advertisers/money), all of the above is the last thing they want to hear.

The fact is that they don't want to be whined at, or preached to, or hear someone (you, your songs) venting about their personal problems. The real world provides that in abundance.

The singer/songwriter is writing his/her own script, to be the person that they invented, that people come to see at 10 o'clock at night.

And it works for them … in that setting.

Just keep in mind that the audience applauding everything you play at 10 o'clock at night in a listening-room environment might be doing so for reasons other than the quality of your songwriting. Let me remind you of the five reasons that the audience "loves your music." I mentioned these at the beginning of the book:

1. Wow, you've got a great personality!
2. Man, you sang the heck out of that song! Gosh you're good.
3. I love this club. I'm so glad we came here tonight.
4. Wow, the wine list is really cool, the beer is cold and the bar snacks are excellent!
5. Man, I like those songs.

But every songwriter longs for a wider audience. That is why our dysfunctional selves do what we do. However, that wider audience wants to hear about themselves. So, unless you are dealing with a descriptive narrative, if you haven't invited the listener in, by the very least at the top of the second verse, the song is history. The singer/songwriter has an venue or performance setting to work in where the audience will sit through song after song that is not about them, and at the end of the night, lavishly praise his/her performance.

Imagine the confusion when radio spurns that singer/songwriter's work as not suitable to hold listeners' attention for 3:30 seconds from the Wally Burger commercial to the Bob's Cleaner commercial at drive time.

Everyone loved them last night, didn't they?

Well, I liked a glass of wine last night. I certainly don't want wine for breakfast. I like Raisin Bran for breakfast, but I don't care for it for dinner.

Finding the Hit Songwriter Inside the Singer/Songwriter

Thankfully, most singer/songwriters choose the more intimate setting. It is their personal preference. My favorite singer/songwriters (yes, I am a huge fan) LOVE playing out at clubs, bars, theaters and looking at their audience. They are humorous, insightful, thought-provoking and reflective. They may not make as much money as "hit radio writers," but in the main they are as happy as the rest of us monumentally dysfunctional creative people can be. Also, every once in a while they may strike gold! They will inadvertently create a radio hit! These hits will be their "calling cards."

Just look at any review of a well-known singer/ songwriter and you will see "so and so," writer of (insert hit song here), played to a full house last night, and so on.

But for the most part, the songs they play in intimate concert settings are scripts for them to be themselves to their fans and indeed ARE "hits" to their audiences.

Aiming for the Charts?
Know Your Two Selves

So, having said all of that, those of you singer/ song-writers who are aiming at the charts have a special burden. You are two people! There is you, the singer, on one side, and you, the writer, on the other side. Now, if the two of you are serious about success, it is essential to be honest about your collective ability to achieve a "hit."

One of you may be great, the other one sucks. You may be a wonderful writer, but a so-so singer, or vice versa.

Don't let one become a donkey for the other.

If you are a brilliant singer but an average writer, don't make the amazing singer that you are perform the ordinary songs that you, the writer, creates. If you're that good of a singer, you can probably make any mediocre song shine.

Conversely, don't give all your wonderful, insightful, humor, irony, detail-laden gems to the second-rate singer that you are.

Now, I will acknowledge that our industry is heavily song-driven … as it should be. Second-rate singers who perform masterfully-written songs will have an easier time getting hits and building a career. On the other hand, great singers with banal, ordinary songs will have a more difficult run to reach the pinnacle of success. I think it is harder to be critical of ordinary songs that are brilliantly performed.

Don't Settle for Mediocrity - Serve the Listener

Great singers ROUTINELY make mediocre songs shine.

Anyone who has co-written with amazing singers will tell you that some artists can make "I love you" sound like you just wrote it for the first time!

The danger here is that instead of being faithful to the listener, we serve the singer. I mean, after all, if the singer likes it and is willing to perform it, isn't that the objective of the exercise? No! The objective of the exercise is to create someone who never existed, in a place that never was, doing something that never happened, and make the listener believe, identify with, and be drawn into your invention in 60 seconds. It is not always to please a singer who is self-absorbed with his/her performance. Unless, of course, you are aiming at "divas" who want big melody and open vowel sounds. But I will touch on that later in the book.

Time to be VERY Honest With Yourself

Always bear in mind that the song is your "pension plan." You want that song recorded, and re-recorded by other artists, put on compilations, sampled, used in movies, commercials, ring tones, singing fish … well, you get the message.

A nice, pleasant, ordinary hit probably won't do the job. So, for a singer/songwriter, aiming at radio, MTV, CMT, BBC, etc. … yours is a particularly slippery slope.

Let me give you views of that slippery slope.

- **Glass empty:** you are not a great singer/ songwriter and your songs are ordinary.
- **Glass half empty:** you are a good singer but your songs are just okay.
- **Glass half full:** your songs are wonderful but you are just a so-so singer.
- **Glass full:** great singer, great writer.

Under the glass empty scenario, if you are possessed by "the fever," at some point you will bitterly acknowledge that you are "ahead of your time," "unlucky," not able to get your material to the "right people," or there is a plot by the entire music industry to prevent you from being "heard." At this point, you go into real estate, rocket science, or brain surgery, etc.

Examining the glass half empty scenario, you'd better cling to the hope that someone you respect will make you see the light and drag you kicking and screaming away from the second-rate songs that are ruining your creative life. With any luck they will find you some great songs, or inject some wonderful songwriters into your world who will give you something brilliant to sing, or co-write with you, in the expectation that you will record, release and have a hit with the resulting collaboration.

Glass half full will work faster if you decide in your infinite wisdom to let other artists record your songs.

But, it has been my experience that if you are a reasonable singer and you want it badly enough, AND you write great songs, you will probably get a record deal after you have a hit … with someone else!

Look on the bright side. At the very least, you will pay your bills and be validated as a creator. To all of us, that is essential.

I don't believe I have to spend much time on the glass full.

Just endure the normal demons and laugh a lot! Remember, the more fun you have, the more money you will make.

NOTES:

CHAPTER 8

CRAFT

SO HOW DO YOU MANAGE to lure the listener in once you've caught their attention and they are coming down the home stretch to "loving it?" That's where craft really comes in.

I told you back in Chapter 2 that this book was not about teaching you how to write songs, but it *is* about teaching you the elements of craft that will make you a *hit* songwriter.

Buckle Up

You have this gift of perception/insight that you are using to tell the world how happy/sad/in love/out of love/smart/stupid/good/bad you are, and wondering why nobody but you and your family wants to sing your songs.

I want you to remember back … back to when you were a consumer rather than a provider of songs. Every song you fell in love to, out of love to, drove your car to, danced to, and so on, was about you or a situation you strongly identified with.

It's Not About You

The writers of those songs gave you "You." They did their job. In the process of doing their job, they demonstrated that they had learned how to get their dysfunctional selves out of the way during the creation of the work and, through the writing process, to give you, you. They offered all the little inclusive details, compounded them with irony, and perhaps some humor, to make you feel totally involved. They invited you into the song and suddenly you, the listener, were on the inside looking out. Well, writer, you have now chosen the job that those great writers did so well for you. You will put food on your table by taking your wonderful gift of perception, forged in dysfunction, and will give the listeners themselves as you see them. As you struggle with this concept, remember, no one sent for you … you picked this profession.

It is All Craft

The parallels between songs and plays, musicals, movies and other entertainment presentations are striking. I have friends who read submitted scripts for major film companies in Los Angeles. They say that they can tell, within a few pages, whether or not a script will make a good movie. Introduction of characters, sub plots occurring in a timely fashion, etc., are essential in engaging the moviegoer. You can load the production with every major superstar in town, and the movie still won't work if viewer expectations are not met. The viewer will not be engaged satisfactorily, ergo, no hit movie! They won't be telling their friends about it.

If You Want a Hit – Craft it Well

The music business is the same as the film business. If the hottest artist on the charts doesn't record potential hit songs that speak to the listener, then that artist doesn't have big hits. A lot of artists, along with their management and record company people, make the mistake of expecting that songs that had people standing on their chairs cheering at 10 o'clock last night are the ones that will engage a listener during drive time the next morning. Another classic mistake happens when the "team" behind the artist assumes (there it is, that "assume" word) that because the artist has had a big "hit," that they can get away with songs that may not be quite as strong as the "hit" was. Not necessarily so!

How Do You Begin?

After the obvious "Don't give up your regular job," there are more tips on songwriting than a golfer has excuses. I'm going to share my best ones with you. All songs have a beginning, a middle, and an end. So, you start at the beginning! As I said before, you create people who never existed, in a place that never was, doing something that never happened, and make the world believe it. You can certainly tell a "true" story if it's really interesting, but never let the truth get in the way of a "good" story or a great song. Make sure you've told the whole story.

Here it is again: a song should have a beginning, a middle, and an end. For an example – you did that, I did this, and now we're doing that and (INSERT YOUR HOOK HERE.)

A hook is the main idea of a song, and usually, but not always, is the song's title. Your job as the songwriter is to lead the listeners step by step through the story and deliver them to the hook – totally involved and completely satisfied. Remember that songs generally are either a dialogue between two people or a narrative simply told. After you've

written your song, look at it all. If you wouldn't have
said it naturally to a lover, friend or enemy the way
it's written, then it probably should be rewritten.
Poems make very boring songs.

Overcoming Writer's Assumption

I've noticed a recurring problem among some of the
writers that I've been critiquing and teaching lately.
I call it "Writer's Assumption." Mr. Webster calls
it "anything taken for granted; supposition," and
believe me, it can be terminal for any song infected
with it. You "assume" the listeners have all the same
information and vision that you have, so you don't
flesh out the characters and the situations. By acting
on that assumption, you have not invited the listener
in. There'll be even more on this in the next chapter.

Listeners Aren't Mind Readers

If a stranger walked up to you on a busy street and
said, "He left her," would you care? The answer,
of course, is no. Well, that's exactly what happens
when you write a lyric that assumes that the listener
knows all about the people who populate your mind.

When you come up with a song idea, characters and
situations immediately spring to life in your head.

So when your pen hits the page, your tendency may be to describe the RESULT of the situation you've just invented in your brain – i.e., "He left her." Your listeners, however, won't care about the result because you haven't created any characters to care about.

Avoid the "Living Room" Syndrome

There's a reason why there are so many "living room" hits. When you sing a song to your friends and family about Uncle Fred joining the Navy, you don't have to explain to them that Fred, who was bitten by a dog, lost his job, and had his foot nailed to the floor by Aunt Martha, who subsequently ran off with an encyclopedia salesman. Because your listeners already know the background of the story, they are prepared to laugh when you sing, "Uncle Fred has a hammock for a bed and makes gravy for the Navy." Any stranger stumbling upon a family laughing hysterically at this ditty would probably consider commitment papers, not publishing contracts.

A Few Rhyme Reasons

As you go through your song's story and the verses, check your rhyme scheme. Whatever it is – change it in your chorus. For instance, change an A B A B rhyme scheme to A B C B .

The reason you do this is to subtly alert listeners that something important is coming. A change in rhyme scheme combined with the change in melody going into the chorus should have them ready for the hook. A couple of effective ways to get the most out of your hook (90 percent of the time, your title is the final line or hook) are to:

1. *Put an internal rhyme immediately preceding the hook line*

For an example, "I love you, you love me too, But we can't make it," or "I hate your dog, he ate my frog, And now I hate you." "And now I hate you" and "But we can't make it" are the lines you intended to emphasize (i.e. your hooks).

2. *Don't rhyme your hook with anything*

A great example of this can be found in Larry Henley's and Jeff Silbar's Wind Beneath My Wings. In their chorus, except for a very subtle implied rhyme with the word "everything," which is tucked in the middle of the second line ("and everything I'd like to be"), the title stands alone. It's also, on examination, made very singable by the use of alliteration. The "W"s in Wind Beneath My Wings really make it soar.

Your First Verse May Not Be the First Verse

Remember, all songs have a beginning, a middle, and an end. Some great old writers beat that into my head 30 years ago. It was the rule then, and it's the rule now. At least 50 percent of the time, when I sit down to write an idea, I mindlessly write the second verse first. Just as I smile in smug satisfaction at a verse well done, the ghost of one of my old mentors jabs me in the brain with a sharp stick and asks, "Well, Shakespeare, just who are these people, and why are they doing this?" Of course, the ghost is right, so I'll write another verse that answers those questions, and I'll make it my new first verse.

Stuck? Try Another Angle

So, for those of you locked in what professional writers know as "second verse hell," remember the tip that a wily old writer told me some years ago. If you've completed your first verse and chorus, and there seems to be nowhere else to go because you've said everything you wanted to say, make the first verse your second verse and write a new first verse (to explain how you got to the second verse). This tip works often enough to make it one of the most valuable tips ever given to me.

Craft Never Goes Out of Style

A lot of things change in 30 years: vocabulary, idioms, situations and attitudes. The craft does not. Making a living from what you love doing is a wonderful thing. One half of love, however, is respect. You'll earn respect by doing your job properly, and your job is to communicate the WHOLE story ... besides, you'll hate that sharp stick I talked about just a little bit ago.

Know When to Quit

Finally, never overwrite. After you've told your story, hit your hook and get out. Too much will always be too much.

Make it Happen in 60 Seconds ... or Less

You have 60 seconds from the start of the song to get the listener's attention. Sixty seconds is a long time. Try sitting quietly for 60 seconds. It can seem endless. So, picture this: in a barely awake, hyper-distracted, seriously-stressed situation, you are definitely not going to indulge anyone or anything that requires input from you, "the listener," for more than 60 seconds. In the real world, probably a tenth of that is all you, "the writer," has to grab your listener.

That 60 seconds rule implies that the listener is listening from the beginning of the song. In most cases they will encounter the song, maybe at the chorus or even the end, and be lured in by the melody or repetition or "sound" of the song. Once they are aware that they might "like" the song, the next time they hear it they will pay attention. It will take a few listens before they ingest it and it becomes "their song" and they "love it," or "it does nothing for them" and "they hate it." Of course, they do neither! What "love," means in this case is that it spoke "*to* them," "*about* them," or is about a situation with which they heavily identify, or not!

I have heard various estimates from radio promotions people and radio station program directors that it takes five to seven listens before a listener really takes a song to heart. I say that you should shoot for eight just to be sure.

Fulfill Expectations

Chekhov asserted that if you put a loaded gun in act one, scene one, you have to fire it before the end of the play. Having created the expectation that something is going to happen, you must honor that commitment! So, when you create an expectation you MUST fulfill it. Throughout the song, you will be creating expectation; and, most of the time, the hook or the title will satisfy that expectation.

Provide Details

Aside from creating an expectation and fulfilling it, detail is one of the songwriter's best friends. For instance, if your title is "That's Why I Love You," I expect to hear a lot of engaging detail leading me toward that title. For example, "Because you wear a purple wet suit and carry a burning chair, and have a parrot on your head … that's why I love you!" Not "we go for a walk, I kiss your lips, you're great … that's why I love you." My dog could write that!

Surprise Me - Lure Me In

If you look at songs like *Right Round* by FloRida, he explains to you to exactly why his head spins right round: "because this woman, there's nothing more beautiful to be found." He's "throwing his money around," and "building castles that are made out of sand."

Jay-Z, in *Empire State of Mind,* is "out of that Brooklyn," and "down in Tribeca," and gives you a whole list of New York goodies.

Carrie Underwood, in her Country song, *Cowboy Casanova,* says "you'd better take it from me, that boy is like a disease," and then lists all the things that make him a Cowboy Casanova.

Don't Be Boring - Don't Assume

Hearing the same banal lyric again and again is not the stuff of enduring copyrights. Get creative, you can say the same thing, but say it with different words.

Engage and Include

Remember, and I repeat, you're creating someone who never existed, in a place that never was, doing something that never happened. It is in your interest to bring your listener up to speed, because if you DON'T include them, they WILL exclude you. All they have to do is push a button or spin a dial. Just remember all of the times when you've been driving along, listening to the radio, when you impulsively

changed stations halfway through a song.
What happened? Well, the writer failed to
engage and hold you.

NOTES:

CHAPTER 9

THE TITLE AND THE NUT

More Craft - Yes, it's *THAT* Important

CRAFT IS ALIVE and well. Songs still reach out to the listeners and work well. They are like "calling cards" that invite listeners to take a closer look. An artist who doesn't write, but who has the ability to choose material well, will reflect his or her depth creating the "legs" that will create careers. Longevity for an artist has always revolved around a song, and that song always has to invite the listener in. And, if they don't write, they are looking to you for "leggy" material.

Titles - Make 'em Original!

The reason that you cannot copyright a title is that the title usually consists of little more than a simple phrase that does not rise to the level of creativity necessary to qualify for its own copyright. Imagine if someone had copyrighted "I Love You" back in 1909. An enormous number of songs would never have been written.

Conversely, an original title like *Pokerface* or *God is Great, Beer Is Good, People Are Crazy,* will likely make the listener curious enough to lend an ear. However, you still can't copyright the title!

The number of title repetitions is worth taking a look at because, as noted before, as a record gets more airplay, the repetitions get more wearing and create a "burn factor." I'll expand more on this later in the analysis section. I'll discuss optimal use of title, and how soon to hear it in the song for maximum rememberability.

Make 'em Easy to Find

Nothing used to drive me crazier than going down to a record store (when there were record stores) and trying to find a copy of a song that didn't feature the title in the hook itself. In the digital age, when you do an online search for a song, it is absolutely necessary that you have sufficient information about that track in order to be able to find it. These days you can't even try singing the song's melody to some long-suffering record store clerk to see if they know which tune you're talking about!

For this reason, when I talk about the hook of the song and the title of the song, 99 percent of the time I am assuming that they are one and the same. The listener is probably only going to remember the catchiest part of the song (the hook), and you want them to be able to hop on their computer, find your song and buy it. That's what this whole music business thing is all about, and we do not want to make the process of buying our songs any more difficult than it absolutely has to be. Remember that, for the time being, there are plenty of ways that they can acquire our songs for free, and if you put your song more than a Google search away from the consumer, there's a good chance they'll never find you.

A song is basically a simple story well told with a memorable melody to lure the listener in, and enough story to hold them. The more melody, the less story; the more story, the less melody. I will explain this later. How you set the listener up, the originality of the idea and the artistic presentation make each song different, not necessarily the originality of the title.

The Hook and the Nut

Back to that old mantra: every song has a beginning, middle and an end. Sounds simple, doesn't it? Well, simple is hard, especially when the song must be so simple that the listener gets it in sixty seconds, and it has the power to hold them for a lifetime.

Every great song has a "hook" – a central idea or theme that I call the "nut." The "hook/nut" is the point, the resolution of the idea, or the conclusion that you lead the listener toward. It is usually positioned prominently, and if you have done your job the listener will not be confused as to what it is.

The "nut" is usually the title of the song as well, so after a listen or two, the audience gets the point of the song. The next few listens are crucial to whether your creation becomes part of the fabric of that listener's life. I repeat myself but you really have only about 60 seconds to invite the listener in and engage them.

So let's begin at the beginning.

The "Nut"

The nut is the conclusion, the point, the message, the result of the story or action.

For a song to be a living thing – sought out by singers, entertaining in elevators, delighting dancers, or making people sing it for 70 years after you're dead – it's important to remember that it must be in perfect balance. A major part of this balance is the ratio of imagery, emotion or story to result.

The reason for this Murphy's Law dealing solely with the "Nut" is that I go through about a hundred songs a week.

At clubs, as I listen to writers in the round or on the half-shell, prepare new writers for their first publishing deal, or help hit writers search for their next publishing deal, I am up to my ears in imagery, emotion and story.

What is missing 90 percent of the time is the essence, the substance, the correct conclusion, the very thing from which mighty oak trees grow ... the Nut.

Origins of the Nut

To put a historical perspective on this process, and to understand the emergence of today's songwriter, let's go back to the dawn of society. There were the hunters, the gatherers, the teachers, the healers, the traders – group after group, scrambling to guarantee its place in the community, its spot near the comfort of the fire.

From a distance, watching the triumphs and failures of human kind, were the storytellers. They were charged with re-creating, bringing to life – with word or gesture – the profound, profane or comic events of society around them. In order to justify their warm place by the fire, they had to entertain, as well as inform. After all, any fool could come back from the hunt and say, "We killed the Woolly Mastodon," but the first one to say, "It was a dark and stormy night as the beast towered above us!" had the audience by the ... ears.

The best of these storytellers, scribes and minstrels became minor celebrities welcome at every fire. Striking the perfect balance between imagery and information, fluff and fact, they generally prospered, thriving on the phrase, "Never let the truth stand in the way of a good story."

That information was passed on from the first song-writer on earth to the second songwriter on earth, who passed it on to Harlan Howard ... at least that's Harlan's story!

Lead the Listener to the Nut

When I'm asked to critique a song, no matter how explicit an idea may appear as I read the lyric or listen to the melody, I always ask the writer one question: "What is this REALLY about?" At least half the time, the answer the writer gives me does not appear anywhere in the song that I have just heard. Therefore, when crafting your songs, make sure that you lead the listener to the Nut (the point you're trying to make), which, many times, is the hook or title of the song.

Three examples follow:

> After references to "It must have been cold there in my shadow," and" You always walked a step behind," Larry Henley and Jeff Silbar lead the listener to the conclusion "If I can fly higher than an eagle," (You are the) *Wind Beneath My Wings.* In this case, the title could be the Nut, but it could also be stated as "your selflessness makes my achievements possible."

> After references to "When I heard that old familiar music start," and "It was like a dam had broken in my heart," Hugh Prestwood leads the listener to "After I'd forgotten all about us." *The Song Remembers When.* In this case, the title could be the Nut, but it could also be stated as "certain songs can trigger certain emotions and memories to make you re-live moments in your life."

> After references to "She could telephone, tell a friend, tell a lie about where she's been," and "send a pigeon, send a fax, write it on a Post-It

pad," Phil Barnhart, Sam Hogin and Mark D. Sanders lead the listener to "I'd prefer a bad excuse to *No News*." (Lonestar, 1996) In this case, the Nut could be stated as "any type of communication from my loved one would be better than none at all."

It's important not to confuse the Nut with the theme. For me, the theme is best expressed in general terms regarding a struggle on a grand scale, such as right vs. wrong, old vs. young, virtue vs. venal, etc. The Nut, however, is the resolution of that struggle.

In addition to being monster hits, each of these songs – as in 99 percent of all hit songs – contains an easily identifiable Nut. In fact, the only exception I can think of is a song like *Unchained Melody*, in which the phrase "unchained melody" occurs nowhere in the song, and the title has no relevance to the song!

Locating the Nut

When searching for the Nut in your own songs, co-writing makes the process easier. To make sure your song is on target, read the lyric aloud and ask your co-writer, "What is this song REALLY about?" At that point, if his or her answer is not clear, re-write. When writing by yourself, finish your song, then on a separate piece of paper write out the Nut in one sentence. Then, the first time you play the song for someone else, ask what he or she thinks the Nut is. If it doesn't coincide with your assessment, you are wrong. Remember, the listener is always right!

Strive for the "Oow" Factor

Judge your songs by what I call the "Oow" factor. Simply put, it means that it's not just a GOOD song; it's SO GOOD that, when you play it for people, they say "Oow!" At that point, you have a perfect song that is in total balance. It uses enough insightful detail to make the situation and the character(s) come to life, but never forgets to perfectly position the Nut: for example, it could be all the reasons that "you are the wind beneath my wings" or that "the song remembers when" or the fact that you can ask anyone you want, but there's still "no news." Once you isolate – and clearly communicate – the "Nut," you'll be welcome at any fire in any cave in the world.

Themes/Premises for Songs Haven't Changed Much Since Adam and Eve

The major themes of love - either lost or found, needed, celebrated, family or country - still dominate most of the popular song repertoire. But no matter how simple, there is always a story well told. As a writer, you will find that there is a major problem when you come up with titles that feel original, striking, or "never heard that before."

You might feel that because the title is so original you can relax lyrically. Wrong. You have to work harder.

Punch Lines Count - Even in Songs

Next time someone tells you a joke that really impresses you, notice that the ingredients of the joke involve not just the punch line. The punch line would be worthless without the proper setup. Ninety percent of what entertains you is the details, the assembly of minor glimpses into the character, the timing and the presentation. What the dog says is as important as the fact that it was said by a dog. Think of your title/hook as the punch line of the song. If you tell the joke badly or fail to set it up properly, the listener won't be there to enjoy the punch line.

Let's Discuss Irony and Humor

The hit songs in all genres from the recent years are filled with an incredible amount of humor and irony. Recent examples are abundant. Country is awash in it.

A Woman Like You, recorded by Lee Brice. When asked by his significant other "What would you do if you'd never met me.?" he responds with, "I'd do a lot more offshore fishing, ...eat a lot more drive-through chicken, take a few strokes of my golf game," and do a lot more beer, pool, poker related things, but.....still be looking for a woman like you."....and, "get sick deep-sea fishing," still have "a hopeless golf game" and don't you know that she "makes the best fried chicken."

Of course Taylor Swift throws some heavy-duty irony in when she talks to the guy with whom she is "never ever ever ever getting back together" when she says that he tells her he "needed space" then comes around and swears he's "gonna change, trust me." Every woman on the planet knows that when a guy tells a woman that he needs "space" or "time to consider his options," he has already moved on, secondly men really aren't that easily capable of change and when they say "trust me" don't!!

Some more irony from Country is Brantley Gilbert's *You Don't Know Her Like I Do.* To a woman, when a relationship ends, it is always the man's fault. So, when he says that his friend "doesn't know her" like he does, obviously he didn't really know her that well! She's gone.

Fun featuring Janelle Monae needs a second "to get my story straight" because his "lover's waiting" for him "just across the bar" but… "when the bar is closing and you feel like falling down," he'll "carry her home!"

Ah yes, the "Irony" of it all.

Looking at humor, you don't have to look far in either Country or Pop. Let's start with *God is Great, Beer is Good, People are Crazy.* You really don't need to go past the title. In *Something About a Truck,* Kip Moore says that "there's something about a girl in a red sundress with an ice old beer pressed against her lips…..will make a boy a mess"' and in *Sexy and I Know It* by LMFAO, it's how he rolls, "animal print, pants out of control" and when he's "at the mall, security just can't fight 'em off." When he's at the beach he's "in a speedo trying to tan my cheeks." Yes, that's how he "rolls."

Where would we be without humor, irony and detail, it is always such a major part of #1 records.

DONT GET LAZY!

In a lot of cases you will …

NOTES:

CHAPTER 10

MORE CRAFT: DETAIL

HAVE YOU EVER BEEN at a party where everybody knows each other and you don't know anyone there?

They are all hugging and laughing and inquiring after, and telling stories about, people you have never met? Unless someone makes an effort to include you in these stories, to give you some background, and to invite you in, you feel excluded. After a while, you leave.

Don't Leave Your Listeners Out

Well, the next time you are listening to a song, riding along in your car or doing something equally distracting and about half way through you reach over and change stations or turn the radio off, it's the same thing as you leaving the party. The writer failed to invite you in, and when you leave the "party," you almost never return.

So you passed on the song. The artist sang well enough, the drums were good, the musicians played well. All the elements were there, except one. The writer failed to engage and hold you. Getting the attention of, inviting in, and holding the listener are the job of the writer. Some of the ways to do all of that are with humor, irony and detail, detail, detail. For example, "That yellow dress you wore on that rusty swing, in the playground by the elm tree, on August 17, made me love you."

Not just a dress, a yellow dress.

Not just a swing, a rusty swing.

In a "playground," not just by a tree but an elm tree, and not just a summer's day, but August the 17th.

Details Matter

In recent Country hits, detail was abundant. In songs like *Feel that Fire* performed by Dierks Bentley, he says "she wants the toy in the Cracker Jack," and to "make every stray a pet." Or, in other examples, two very successful artists, Keith Urban and Brad Paisley, say they wanted to get their "picture in the hometown paper" (*Start A Band* performed by both Urban and Paisley), or "buy their mommas a Cadillac" (*Start a Band*), or "borrow Uncle Jake's Mustang" (*Sweet Thang*/Urban), or check out her "trusty rusty had a flat" (*It Happens* performed by Sugarland).

Just hearing Taylor Swift envying some other girl and saying, "she's Cheer Captain, and I'm on the bleachers," is worth the price of admission (*You Belong With Me*).

And, of course, Pop music is awash with detail. *Single Ladies* begins with the line "up in the club, we just broke up," and by the end of the first verse we've found out the background on the relationship as Beyonce cried her tears and "gave three good years," and every woman out there agrees that "he should have put a ring on it." And we cheer because the new guy is holding her tighter than her Dereon jeans.

Lady Gaga, in *Just Dance,* can't find her "drink or man." She's also lost her keys or phone, can't remember the name of the club she's in, but she'll be okay as long as she can "just dance."

In *Fireflies,* Owl City is hanging out with "10 million fireflies" that "leave teardrops everywhere," "try to teach him to dance," "a foxtrot" above "his head," and "a sock-hop beneath his bed."

Don't Get Lazy

It's so easy to go through all the hit songs in all genres from past years and find incredible amounts of detail. In a lot of cases you will inadvertently create your own opportunity to set the stage through that aforementioned "writer assumption."

"Writers assumption" is considered by most to be a bad thing. I, on the other hand, view it as an opportunity. I talked about this earlier in Chapter 7, and I'm hammering it into your head again. Don't lose your listener because you forgot the details.

When you get a great idea for a song, in the few seconds it takes to find a scrap of paper and something to write with, you will already have created the characters in your mind. You know how they met, who they are, what they are wearing, everything about them.

In your mind the story is moving along toward the wonderful "nut/hook" you are zeroing in on. Your pen, pencil, crayon, or computer hits the road at that point of the action. It will probably not have occurred to you that the wealth of background information in your head has not been communicated to the listener.

You have excluded them. In defending the indefensible, a lot of writers trot out the oldest chestnut in the GREAT BOOK OF WRITER'S EXCUSES.

"I like to leave it to the listener's imagination!" Come on...

Many times, I will be listening to someone's demo and about halfway through the second verse I find myself looking at the wall and thinking, "Wallpaper! This room could use some wallpaper!"

Oops.

The song is still playing, and I am totally disengaged from it.

What that means is that the writer failed. They didn't give me the information (read: "Detail") or background to interest me in their story. The writer assumed that I would intuitively understand all the background information that would make their characters and story as fascinating for me as it was for them.

The listener has no imagination.

I am a writer, and I'm not going to fill in the blanks of your song for you! Okay, maybe I'll let you fill me

in if I'm sitting on my couch with a glass of wine and
you tell me what it's all about at 10 o'clock at night,
but certainly not at 7 a.m. when I'm in my car.
Writer's assumption can be negative; but if you
know you're going to do it, consider it a gift.

NOTES:

CHAPTER 11

YES, EVEN MORE CRAFT

Second Verse Curse

HOW MANY TIMES have you written a verse and chorus and anguished over the second verse.

But ... you've said everything there is to say. It's all there in the first verse you have written.

You have said it all. You then enter what is called "second verse hell." Get over it.

It's a very normal thing to write the second verse first. And what it does is provide you with a wonderful opportunity to create a detail-rich, inviting first verse. You simply move that verse you just wrote thinking it was the first verse and make it the second verse.

After that, you can look very candidly at where you are taking the listener, and then lead them where you want them to go.

If you want to get a mule to go where you want it to go and you give it the option of a carrot or a stick, you will find that the carrot wins every time. Once you know you are going to do something stupid like write the second verse first, you can turn that knowledge to your advantage.

Melody and Lyrics Must Work Together

You will notice now that we have started looking at crafting songs, that I spend a disproportionate amount of time focusing on lyrics. In a lifetime of observation, I have noted that what lures the listener to a song is melody, but what keeps them involved are the lyrics! To me the keeping is the hard part. And I know I'll get a lot of heat from my composer friends for that!

A couple of years ago, I was fortunate to be paired with John Capek, a wonderful melody man who was also a great teacher. The Songwriters Association of Canada sent us out on a multi-city teaching trip. In watching his approach to craft, I got a sense of how to verbalize what the composer expects from the lyricist. Simply put, when you, the composer, are dealing in major chords, you, the lyricist, are generally setting up a very clear statement. The listener expects you to be direct and set up the story/hook in a strong unambiguous way.

When the listener hears minor chords from the composer, he/she is inclined to think "sad" and/or "wistful." So, you, the lyricist, must give them sad and wistful. Major 7ths are a little more candles and wine, long walks and holding hands. So again, when you are creating a composition that relies heavily on major 7ths, you will need to lyrically fulfill the listener's expectations.

Diminished chords change the dynamic in the song and provide the lyricist with a questioning "hey what's happening" opportunity.

Augmented chords will set the stage for something about to occur. Don't let them down!

The catchiest part of the melody and the lyrical fulfillment of the expectation (the hook, the nut) usually occur at the same time. That is the part that first-time or second-time listeners will have found appealing enough to pay attention to the next time they hear it. Over their next few exposures they will assimilate the song. And again, after 8-10 listens or so, they will make a subconscious decision of either "I love that song," or "I hate that song." And again, of course, they neither "love" nor "hate" the piece of work. What they mean is that the work will engage them, hold them and speak to them - *about* them - every time they hear it.

Crossing Genres - Still *More* Craft

During my professional career, I have had hits in different genres by doing my homework. Once you research what craft is used in a specific genre, then you must immerse yourself in the vocabulary and technology of that genre. The craft is your foundation. In crossing genres, vocabulary and technology are major variables. For writers successful in one genre, making the transition to another is challenging, but doable.

The major thing I had to analyze in each genre in which I worked was:

- What was the expectation of the audience?
- What was the time of day they were listening?
- What were the circumstances under which they experienced the song?
- What was the vocabulary that they commonly used?

So I had to learn a new way to use language for each genre that I entered. One of the most important things I did was find co-writers who were familiar with the language of the genre. That, for me, was one of the major benefits of co-writing.

As a part of the process of immersing myself in a new genre, I also had to learn the technology that they used. For example, when I worked in Pop, I was thoroughly familiar with it. I had toured with a lot of Pop acts like the Walker Brothers, the Kinks, and Martha and the Vandellas, etc. When I moved to New York, I listened to an awful lot of Rock and Roll and produced the early Max's Kansas City compilations, which gave me the expertise I needed in order to effectively produce acts like April Wine. I had to have a good sense of Rock, but I also brought my Pop sensibilities to the sessions, producing them as Rock acts doing Pop songs.

Then I started doing R&B, working with Chris Bartley, Donnie Elbert, the 3 Ounces of Love, the Platters, etc. Again, I had to learn all the common practices for that new genre. Thankfully, I had met some major artists and producers and became very much a student of the music they created as well as the music of the Flamingos and different street-corner bands. So I got a really great one-on-one education from the New York Rhythm and Soul community.

The truly fantastic result of having studied those different styles of music is that I can now return to those genres and feel comfortable once I learn the current "language" that is being used. For example, as an extension of my work with April Wine, I had some cuts with a group called Annihilator, a thrash metal band. I looked at their audience, their vocabulary, what they were talking about, and was able to have some pretty productive writing sessions with Jeff Waters, their producer and lead guitarist.

However, I did recognize my limitations, and I knew when to go looking elsewhere for the best song for the acts I was producing. When you're wearing two hats - both as writer and a producer - your first obligation is to seek out the best possible material for the band to record, and that material may not necessarily be your own.

Will They Buy It?

With all this talk about title, verses, rhyming, nuts, details, genres and prosody, it still comes down to: will your listener lay down some hard cash or plastic to buy your tunes? And, will they play it over and over? And will they tell their friends about it?

I love Cajun music. I love Bluegrass music. Whenever there is a great band nearby, I make a point to go and listen. I genuinely love creative dance songs.

I usually buy the CD.

When I get home I almost never play it!

Because . . .

The music that held me so completely the night before did its job in the setting it was designed for. It is unrealistic to expect it to turn my crank when I'm trying to balance my checkbook!

Look at horses, some run brilliantly in the rain. They call them "mudders." Well, you don't bet on a "mudder" on a dry day. The old saying, "the race is not always won by the swiftest or most fleet of foot … but that's the way to bet," has always rung true.

NOTES:

CHAPTER 12

THE MIGHTY PRONOUN

The Little Big Word

MANY TIMES, in trying to get the listener's attention, writers will fixate on song-crafting devices such as story, story development, metaphor, alliteration and imagery, while forgetting to pay attention to the little personal pronouns. *HE, SHE, IT, THEY, THEM, US, WE, I, YOU, and ME* may not look like much, but they define who does what to whom. They also can affect the writer's marketablity and, therefore, the value of his or her work.

First- and Second-Person: The Favorites

When seized by an idea, most male writers, upon sitting down to sketch out a scenario for a song, almost automatically start off with: "She did or said this or that." For women, it is often: "He did this or that." Once the character and the type of relationship evolve, it often becomes necessary to change the pronoun. For instance, if the song describes an intense, one-on-one relationship between the singer and another person, the pronouns used are a first- and second-person: *YOU, I, ME, US* and *WE.* This frees the third-person pronouns *HE, SHE, IT, THEY, THEM* to be used as outside influences that complement or come between, *YOU, I, ME, US,* and *WE.* For an example, "I love *YOU,* but *THEY* say that we can't make it." The song becomes more personal when *YOU* and I are used.

Third-Person is Best in Some Cases

Remember that songs are vehicles for singers who want to communicate with their audiences. When an artist leans over the footlights, and sings "I love *HER*" – who cares? But if the message is "I love *YOU*" – a rapport is established.

Some exceptions to the rule are as follows: If the song is about a total loser, it will definitely be third-person: *HE* or *SHE.* No star is going to stand on stage and describe himself or herself as a jerk unless it is so tongue-in-cheek that the listeners know that it's a joke.

At seminars or new writers' nights, I often hear songs in which the singer is supposed to be a grandparent. Wrong! If you want to get a song like that recorded, it has to be third-person: "Good old Grandpa, *HE* was... " or "Good old Grandma, *SHE* did... " In the business of grooming artists, image is everything. The words "youthful" to "mature" are used to describe performers with a record deal. You only become old when you get cold and no major label will touch you with a barge pole.

When a relationship is really over forever, the pronoun is third person: *HE* or *SHE*. For an example, "*SHE'S* about as gone as a girl can get." If any love or hope lingers, however, then the pronoun will be second person: *YOU*. For an example, "I know *YOU'RE* gone forever, but in *MY* heart ... " (I refer to this as the "Bozo Finds Love And Won't Let Go" syndrome. It has been observed that Bozo the Clown and people in love sometimes have a lot in common.)

When the singer performing the song is using the audience as a confidante or is telling a friend about a great relationship, it's third-person: *SHE* or *HE*. For an example, "*He's* so wonderful."

When one of the characters in a *HE* or *SHE* song has a conversation with someone within the song, the pronoun can switch to second-person: *YOU*. For an example, in John Ims' *She's In Love With The Boy*,

Mama says in the third verse: "My Daddy said YOU wasn't worth a lick." In The Beatles' *She's Leaving Home*, they go to "*WE* gave *HER* all of our love."

Fight to Avoid Switching

The only really major no-no in the use of pronouns occurs when the characters are third-person (*HE* or *SHE*) in the verse then suddenly switch to first- or second- person (*YOU, I* or *ME*) in the chorus, or vice versa. I would imagine that any writer worth his or her salt would have seen that information written in block letters three feet tall and underlined in red, so I won't go into that any further.

Pronouns Matter - I Repeat

In order to lure me, the listener, in, the smartest tactic is to speak *to* me, not *about* me. Though I dealt with the pronoun issue previously (the little big word), we're going to go over it again. Let me remind you that when it comes to the song as a script, the pronoun is the little *huge* word. If I'm your listener (a woman), you'll get my attention faster if the song is about *You, Us* or *We*. If the song is about *Her, Him* or *Them,* you must work much harder to capture and keep my (womanly) interest.

Target Practice - Image

Even if your pronoun use is correct, if the song is using the first-person pronoun (*Me, I, We,* etc.) and the central figure is too old, too young, or not cool enough, you won't hit the bulls-eye when you try to pitch it. So, if the story still begs to be told, and you have a fresh way to say it, and if the song is just not quite the first-person image that the artist, management or label wish to project, you might consider changing to the third-person pronoun in your script, although the change will decrease the odds that your song will make it to #1. For example, the artist can sing the off-image song (the song's character is a homeless drunk, perhaps, and the artist is an observer, not the main character) without it reflecting personally on him or her.

Ready, Aim, Fire – Bulls-eye

Also, by employing third-person pronouns, you double the number of artists in your pitch arc, your bulls-eye zone. Male and female artists have equal credibility when they sing a third-person song. And, if the message and language are consistent with what their audience expects from them, everybody wins. How about this? Guess how much your publisher will love you when you come in with a song that can be pitched to pretty much any artist out there!

If you're going to go with third-person, the message has to be universal and the writing has to be first-rate.

Third-Person Exceptions to the Rule

Another more subtle reason to use third-person is to indicate to the listener (the woman, remember?) that a relationship is really, really over (or the lesson very well learned) and that the singer has moved on. Consider this example using first-person and second-person pronouns, *I, You:* "I know that you're gone forever, but I'll always love you." By saying this, the singer is subtly telling the audience that the candle is still in the window. The heart hasn't let go even if the words say so.

When you use the third person - *He, She, Them* - you are making it clear that the relationship is over and you're ready to move on. For example, "I know he's gone, we had some good times, but I've got my eye on some brand new guys."

Third-Person Caution Zone

You can be complimentary or express affection for the now-gone him or her in your song, but be careful!

Don't be too warm in your reverie or paint too glowing of a picture of just how great that person (she) in
your life was, otherwise, you create the suspicion in
the new "you" in your life, that woman listener, that
there is still some ambivalence about the old relationship. A wishy washy message leads the listener
to view the singer as, at the very least, not quite
trustworthy.

Just try describing an old love in glowing terms to
your current significant other and be prepared for a
lifetime of that story being brought back up to you
again and again at the strangest times.

As a matter of fact … probably even as your casket
is being lowered into the ground!

Pronouns and Hits - Country

But more typically, we will find first person
pronouns dominating in hit songs. If we take a
look at what happened at #1 in Country music in
2009, *Cowboy Casanova* used the third person *him*
while talking to *you* allowing Carrie Underwood
to caution her pal, "that boy is like a disease," and
"the devil in disguise," and "you'd better run for
your life." However, using third person pronouns,
She's Country allowed Jason Aldean to (1) cover
the country virtues of every woman from South

Carolina to Kansas, (2) be inclusive, and (3) not exclude any southern woman of any age or location from his celebration. *It Won't Be Like This For Long*, in the third person, allowed Darius Rucker to walk us through what it's like to be a father without personally having to be one.

More hits in first person (*I, Me*), talking about third person (*Him, Her, She* and *Them*), which allowed the singer to extol third-person virtues are: Toby Keith's, *God Love Her*, and in Dierks Bentley's, *Feel That Fire*, or tell a great story in Billy Currington's, *People Are Crazy*.

Over 50 percent (16 of 31) of Billboard Country #1s were first person (*You, Me, I, Us, We*) which is in line with country songs being a linear, lyrical conversation between two people – *you* and *me*.

Pronouns and Hits - Pop

In Pop, at #1 on the Billboard Charts, a lot of the songs were scripts that involved multiple performers, e.g. Black Eyed Peas, Eminem, etc. The songwriters still used first person pronouns along with *he, she, it, they, him* and *them*. The impact of using the pronoun, *you*, cannot be overstated. When *I*, as the songwriter (and, by extension, the artist), am speaking to *you*, the listener, it is a direct invitation to *you*,

the listener, to engage with the song rather
than simply be a passive listener.

NOTES:

CHAPTER 13

INTRODUCTION TO THE SIX FORMS

NOW, LET'S GET INTO analyzing some of the different "forms," "shapes," or "outlines" that are used by professional songwriters. I refer to them as "forms" because when I teach, after you learn what the forms are, it makes it easier for me to give you a number/form that is specific to your song, to avoid confusion.

As I have stated, as far as I'm concerned it takes the radio listener an average of eight listens to ingest and assimilate and understand the song, and once they have done that they make the decision to "love it" or "hate it."

Part of the reason they love it or hate it, is that, as a structure or outline or shape, it behaves like the listener expects it to behave. The song offers up the idea and then delivers it exactly where the listener expects it to be.

Song Structures

There are six basic shapes or forms of the popular/ hit song. Within the framework of each of these shapes/forms you can expand or contract the section, whatever you choose to call those sections (i.e. verse, bridge, middle eight, channel, lift, climb, chorus, pre-chorus, etc.), to suit your need to tell your story.

Just for the sake of clarity, the verse is generally where you set up the premise of the song. It can be four, six, eight lines or more. The lift or climb or channel or pre-chorus or any one of a dozen names this particular section has (e.g. in Europe it is referred to as a bridge) is two, four, six lines that precede the title or chorus of the song. Generally it changes rhyme scheme from the verse and creates tension by implying or actually using the words "but," "maybe," "when," "because," etc., and then in most cases it lifts the listener melodically to the chorus or title.

The chorus which, incidentally, comes from the Greek "khoros" which means a group of singers, is essentially the destination to which you have been leading the listener. Remember that most people do not sing very well but will feel comfortable singing along with a large group of other people. Once they do that, they will genuinely feel as they are a part of your song and are much more involved and even feel a sense of ownership of the song. The middle eight, or the bridge as it is called in the United States, is a part that is musically different, has a different rhyme scheme, and has two functions.

It is noted for showing information not included in the body of the song or demonstrating contrast, for example, "but" or "what if. " Also, it need not be eight bars long. It can be six, ten, twelve bars - whatever works for you. It is generally positioned after the second chorus, possibly before or after an instrumental.

Moving along, you must give me a story somewhere, no matter how lightweight. So if all your weight/story is in the chorus, you only need a light verse to set it up.

Conversely, when you are telling the bulk of your story in the verse, your resolution in the chorus can be fairly simple.

No matter how you alter the structure from within, you must remain faithful to the intent of the structure. What that means is that after you have led me, the listener, into a form, I will expect you to at least vaguely remain in that form.

If you suddenly change, you will divert my attention from the message of the song; and any distraction, even momentary, can spell disaster.

Remember, you don't have hours to engage and keep me. You only initially have about 60 seconds, if you're lucky.

FIRST FORM

First Form is a wonderful old form used a lot in the '30s, '40s and '50s. It still can be found in musical theater occasionally and the songs of that era are still performed in clubs and theatres and musical reviews. We don't hear a lot of songs in First Form on radio today simply because "hit" radio hated it. The song started with what was called a verse and it then went into a chorus or refrain. Because the verse was generally different in tempo from the chorus/refrain, radio had a problem with it so they clipped it off!

Therefore, in most cases today, we are only aware of the chorus/refrain. There are exceptions to this, think *I Left My Heart In San Francisco* or *Rudolph the Red Nosed Reindeer*. In both cases these songs are performed intact simply because they are enduring standards. Many others survive only in chorus/refrain mode. My mentors, who were writers during the '40s and '50s, wrote extensively in this form and were big fans of this form. They explained how the creative process and the "business" worked together.

Back then the publisher was like a benevolent dictator, and writers would have to keep office hours. They would sit in airless rooms with pianos, until they came up with an outline for a song.

This outline would generally be the chorus or refrain part we know today.

They would rush out of their cubicles and play the chorus/refrain for the publisher. If the publisher thought it was a "good idea," the writer would be told to "finish it."

"Finish it" basically meant write the verse. The verse would set up the song.

In the case of *Rudolph the Red Nose Reindeer,* this section told you who Rudolph was, simply because he had not existed prior to being created in this song. We all knew about Dancer and Prancer, etc. so the verse was essential to introduce this brand new character.

Look at *I Left My Heart In San Francisco.* If you exclude the front part (verse) you leave the listener without a vital piece of information. The first line of the chorus/refrain says, "I left my heart in San Francisco," which tells the listener that the singer was somewhere other than in San Francisco.

The verse fulfills two functions. It contrasts where the singer has been traveling, to the place he calls home. First, it states where the singer is now and why he was wise to pine for San Francisco. I mean, Paris was sad, Rome didn't ring his bell, and he was alone and forgotten in Manhattan, so we understand his longing to get home especially since he paints such a loving picture of San Francisco. Putting the beginning on these songs completely satisfies the listener's need to know. This form worked brilliantly for writers because most writers write the second verse first anyway.

Remember when you get that wonderful idea for a song, by the time you find a pencil and paper or boot up, you have created the characters in your mind.

So you start from a point in the story that's slightly down the road.

This form that I have designated first form allows the writer to address that problem. It was the perfect solution to "writer's assumption" and "second verse hell"!

Other examples of First Form are Cole Porter's *I Get a Kick Out of You* and Hoagy Carmichael's *Stardust*.

SECOND FORM

Second Form is used a lot in Rock and Roll and also as an expanded version in Folk and Urban. The goal is always to lead the listener to the hook or nut (read title). Remember, you, the writer, control how that listener is lead.

Well, Second Form is really all about the musicianship of the artist and the great chorus/hook that makes the song a sing-along anthem. For musicianship you must also consider the production values. Low-cost digital recording equipment has enabled most musicians to really polish the sound of their recordings. As a matter of fact, it is entirely possible to have a not very well-written song be successful in spite of its flaws just because it was brilliantly produced.

It is basically verse, chorus, verse, chorus, instrumental, chorus, chorus out.

In the rock version of this form you will hear a dominant musical riff that you will identify with the song. Think *Satisfaction* by the Rolling Stones or *Maybelline* by Chuck Berry.

In its Rock form it is an excellent vehicle for rock and roll and metal because of its simplicity. A recent example of a Rock usage of this form can be found on Linkin Park's *Shadow of the Day*.

In Country music we find Second Form used by Ashley Gorley, Dallas Davidson and Jeremy Stover on *Start a Band* which was performed as a duet by Keith Urban and Brad Paisley. In Rap, Eminem used it to good effect on his song, *Crack a Bottle,* which also featured Dr. Dre and 50 Cent. Another parallel between the songs was the use of an introductory section which sets up a premise. In *Start a Band,* the guitarists play guitar licks from classic rock songs, and Eminem used the opening of his song to introduce himself as his Slim Shady persona. Both of those songs borrow somewhat from the First Form before launching into the Second Form.

For all of the examples above, you should pay attention to the amount of detail that the writers used in order to keep the listener engaged throughout the song.

For radio there is usually no third verse after the instrumental. If you as a writer feel the need for more information (if your verses are short, then tuck a second verse right after the first verse, before the first chorus.)

The third verse will then become the verse after the first chorus.

Confused? Well here is the diagram for this form V, (Verse optional), C, V, C, INST, C, C, C Etc.

THIRD FORM

Third Form is really a more complicated second form but allows the writer to take a different emotional approach. You lead the listener much differently in this form. As in all cases, it is important to invite the listener into the story, as a participant wherever possible or as an involved observer at the very least. (See prior chapter on pronouns.) The Third Form, by adding a bridge or middle eight to its structure, invites and encourages the listener to look a little harder at the story, by showing another side to the story. The best way to describe the function of the bridge or middle eight is that it provides information not included in the body of the song or provides contrast. So, when you approach writing the middle eight or bridge, think "but, what if?"

The bridge/middle eight at radio not only shows the other side of the story and provides new information, it can also be used to highlight the message of the song. The middle eight or bridge can be two lines, four lines, six lines, whatever you want it to be. But whatever it is, make your point and get the listener back to the chorus. Most of the big songs in this form almost never have a verse after the middle eight. You can have an instrumental before or after the middle eight if the spirit moves you, but no verses. And again, like Second Form, if you feel you need more story, tuck another verse in before the first chorus. If you feel a need for more story, then in all probability, the verses you have are fairly short and even with the extra verse, you will still arrive at your hook/title in about 60 seconds.

Some good examples of usage of this form would be *My Life Would Suck Without You* written by Max Martin, Dr. Luke and Claude Kelly, and performed by Kelly Clarkson in the Pop genre. In Country we see it on *Here Comes Goodbye* written by Chris Sligh and Clint Lagerberg, and performed by Rascal Flatts; or *Then* written by Chris DuBois, Ashley Gorley and Brad Paisley, and performed by Brad Paisley.

On the song, *Single Ladies,* you can see how flexible this form is in that the writers added a call and response section which is used both at the beginning and the end where they shout out to all the single ladies. This takes a basic Third Form song and adds a new dimension to it.

In Country music, Third Form was, by far, the most popular structure used with 17 out of the 31 total number one songs in 2009 employing this form.

FOURTH FORM

Fourth Form adds yet another dimension to the writer's creative freedom. In addition to a bridge/ middle eight we have a wonderful little section that is sometimes called a bridge in Europe but is usually called the lift, climb, pre-chorus or channel by American songwriters. This new section has a very specific function at radio. I chose to call it a lift because that is usually how it functions musically. It generally lifts the listener melodically into the chorus. It is two, four, sometimes six lines that not only lift the listener (think launch the listener toward the hook, title or chorus) but is a place where you can also create a little tension.

On examination, you will find that hit writers position an "if, maybe, and, but, when, why," in the lift that is quickly resolved by the hook/chorus. (Create tension, resolve it.) Traditionally, there was no middle eight or bridge in Fourth Form, although it can still happen in its original form, i.e., *The Climb,* written by Jessi Alexander and John Mabe, and performed by Miley Cyrus.

After the second chorus, there would be an instrumental over the melody of the verse with the vocals re-entering on the lift or the chorus. Again, give no new information after that last chorus. However, in the interest of flexibility and the need to accommodate radio, it has become common not only to have new information in each of the lifts but to add a middle eight or bridge.

So, you have, if you are a lyricist, up to three distinct sections, each with their own possibilities for engaging the listener in a slightly more complicated story line than any other form/shape. An excellent example of this is *Love Song* written and performed by Sara Bareilles. As a lyricist she takes maximum advantage of the working space that the structure offers her by providing new information on each of the lifts that occur within the song. She also has a small middle eight or bridge and finally she adds new information in the closing choruses to keep the listener engaged and hold them until the end of the song. Alternately, Leona Lewis's song *Bleeding Love* which was written by Jesse McCartney and Ryan Tedder re-uses the same lift or climb consistently throughout. With all the freedom this structure provides to add new information in each section, you have to be careful not to overwrite it!

You will notice a subtle difference in forms two, three and four that have everything to do with audience expectation. Second Form is a very young, angst, anger, party, rooted form that gets to the point very quickly and in tandem with the almost 50/50 input of a dominant musical riff has a very fast, audience performance connection.

Adding the lyrical middle eight or bridge to the Third Form adds a questioning, or additional informational aspect to the song that requires slightly more thought from the listener. The listener has to do more than simply respond on a primary level. Fourth Form demands an investment from the listener. First, there is the statement of the premise, then the question of the premise in the pre-chorus or additional information, then the resolution of the idea. Add to that the potential to have a middle eight or bridge as well as some new information in the choruses, and you have a lyrical challenge both as a writer and a listener.

FIFTH FORM

In the Fifth Form we find the old trusty AABA. In traditional AABA, the A parts are verses and the B section is the bridge. There is no sing-song chorus. This form is characterized by its lack of a chorus. The first or last line of each verse of A section holds the title of the song. Think *Brown Eyed Girl* as well as *See You Again,* written by Tim James, Destiny Cyrus, Antonina Armato, and performed by Miley Cyrus; and *Yesterday,* written by Paul McCartney, and performed by the Beatles. All writers seem to lay claim to having used this form. From Muscle Shoals to Manhattan and around the world there is tremendous affection for this form. It is, however, quite deceptive in its simplicity, and a major component of this form is melody. This immediately creates a problem.

Given our preference, the human animal will, when given the option, always defer to melody. Unfortunately, we are not very good at sonically multi-tasking. Some would say that we don't at all. What attracts us to a song is always melody, but what keeps us there is a lyric. I've heard people say that they only hear melody, and they really don't care about the lyrics. Well, if you play them the song it's amazing how they seem to know the words.

How does the writer achieve telling the story and engaging the listener melodically? With great difficulty! Remember, where you tell your story you remain linear. It's been said that you don't change your chord until you change your thought. As an illustration, rap cannot coexist with melody, as there is so much information imparted in the verses that there really is not a lot of room for melody. However, as we watch the evolution of rap, we hear the introduction of melody (i.e. samples of the melodic segments of well-known songs) to engage the listener and attract new listeners.

Anyway, back to AABA. Aside from melody, the major feature that will engage the listener is the sense of time passage or chronology, i.e., if you think of the first verse as the "in the beginning" or "once upon a time" verse, the second as the "here and now" verse, the bridge as new information, the other side of the story or sometimes just simply the message of the song, and the third verse as the "on down the road" or "when we're old and gray" verse, then you won't go far wrong. Just in case you were wondering when I will be addressing the cousin to AABA, the AAAA, etc. —

I won't be. I need to keep this book from becoming too big. You could suggest that AAAA is really the seventh form, and I am always reminded how much fun the form was. However the word is "was." I am dealing with what makes money in the current music business, and has the most potential to become a standard and go on making money long after you are in your rocking chair.

There are some AAAAs that do well in Rap and Hip-Hop, and it will always be a beloved Folk music form. Always be aware that forms/structures are always in a state of flux. Nothing radical, but the changes are always market-based.

I am always impressed when a writer adds or deletes parts of structure and has a monster hit. For instance, on the 2009 Pop charts, if you look at *Fireflies* written by Adam Young and performed by Owl City, the song hews roughly to the Fifth Form. It incorporates a sort of chorus but, otherwise, honors all the standard conventions of Fifth Form.

The only #1 song written in Fifth Form in Country was *God Is Great, Beer Is Good, People Are Crazy*, and it stayed true to the fundamental structure of the Fifth Form.

In most cases it will be really good writers who will follow their heart, go off on a tangent and let the song beginning, middle and end unfold the way the story leads. That simplicity is generally achieved by someone with a high awareness of craft who just lets a great idea evolve and involves the listener from beginning to end.

SIXTH FORM

My pal Harlan Howard called this the "honky tonk" form. I am convinced that Harlan believed that God created the Honky Tonk so that Adam and Eve would have a place to go after they got bounced from the Garden of Eden.

Well, it has been around for long time. In classical music it was known as the rondeau, and in the Jazz clubs of the 1930s and 40s it was called "rondo." It was also used frequently in Western Swing.

After examining the last couple of hundred years of songwriting, it is no surprise that songs lyrically and structurally adapt to the expectation of the listener. In his book, *Side Man,* W.O. Smith mentions this form was used to good effect to get people up on the dance floor quickly. In fact, if you look at most major dance records they use at least a portion of the chorus at the front of the song to create an expectation that the listener is going to be dancing pretty quickly! The major feature of the rondo/rondeau/honky tonk/Sixth Form is that it moves the listener into the meat of the song very quickly.

Its chorus, verse, chorus, musical turnaround/instrumental, bridge/middle eight, chorus, etc., structure is a very no-nonsense, get-to-the-point, here-it-is, the "let's get it on" approach to a song.

One of the many appealing things about this form from a live performance standpoint is the musical turnaround/instrumental section that followed the chorus/verse/chorus and allowed the band to stretch out and gave each band member the opportunity to play a solo. After everyone has had a chance to shine, instead of going back into a chorus, we are swept into the bridge/middle eight which was a whole new section musically and lyrically.

This satisfies the listener and then pumps you back into the chorus. Theoretically, in this form, you could include new information in the choruses, maybe even go mad and repeat the bridge/middle eight with some new information, who knows? Whatever you do, have fun. The more fun you have – as long as you carry the listener with you – the more enduring the story.

A couple of good illustrations of this form are: *Good Morning Beautiful* written by Zachary Lyle and Todd Cerney, performed by Steve Holy, as well as *Ain't No Mountain High Enough,* written by Nicholas Ashford and Valerie Simpson, and performed by the writers among many others. Modified versions of the form are regularly used in Dance music. It generally creates the expectation in the listener that they are going to get up and dance.

ANOMALIES

Before you bombard me with the fact that your favorite artist had huge success with a fifteen-minute-long song with no chorus, no second verse, and never mentions the title anywhere in the body of the song, I know. As a matter of fact, when Roger Cook and I started Picalic Music, the first hit we published that Roger and Bobby Wood had co-written was *Talking in Your Sleep.* It had no second verse. It did, however, end up as a #1 Country record, a Top 10 Pop record and BMI's Song of the Year the following year. I had them write a second verse which was never used, but for some reason the song satisfied the listener and did its job. In the final analysis, if the song satisfies the listener, that's a good thing. As a matter of fact, it's the only thing!

You will be barraged with records that structurally don't seem to fit listener expectations. However, in an MTV, ADD, internet world where 5 to 10 seconds is an eternity, the casual listener will accept a lot of departures from craft if reinforced by video, beats-per-minute for dancing, fashion, attitude and repetition. You will see pronouns and rhyme schemes change from section to section and all sorts of other liberties being taken by songwriters, particularly in Pop.

One of the many ways it is made acceptable is by having multiple personalities on a record. A great deal of the time, there will be a major act featuring another act; or, in cases like the Black Eyed Peas, the group works as an ensemble with each member of the group expressing their individuality through their allotted section of the song.

You've heard me say that the listener is always attracted by melody. A major and obvious anomaly which absolutely contradicts that assertion but which has been a major force in Pop music would seem to be Rap.

As I have mentioned in articles and when I teach, I watched, many years ago, as Rap became a major staple of Popular music, and wondered how long it would take for the creators of these works to get beyond the first glow of novelty and have to invite the listener in by using melody.

It was fascinating to watch. Not just because samples of familiar songs were being incorporated into Rap songs, but also because the producers were adding choruses with memorable melodies to attract the listener. The reason for this, of course, is that melody and lyric are mutually exclusive. Had they introduced melody with the Rap, the listener would have diverted their attention to the melody and missed a lot of the detail in the Rap. This combination has allowed a very comfortable alliance between Rap and conventional song structure.

As music evolves, I am always surprised by new twists that songwriters and producers come up with to push the craft of songwriting into uncharted territory. As I discover new things I will keep passing them on to you. It's been a great trip so far.

NOTES:

CHAPTER 14

QUICK RECAP

SO, WE'RE A BAKER'S DOZEN chapters into this, and that last one was a doozy. Let's take a little breather and recap some of the most important points so far. And I'll sprinkle in some singability issues to keep you on your toes.

The Song As a Script

If you're a stand-alone writer, the song you write is a script for artists to have a conversation with their listeners (women, remember?).

Each listener must feel singled out and special. Remember, this is all about the listener.

You will use your songwriting gift to provide artists with the vehicle that they need to give themselves to listeners.

Artists As Performers

The major difference between actors and singers is that most actors can change characters from film to film, whereas, successful singers rarely depart radically from the image they have chosen.

That presents the stand-alone songwriter with hurdles that require careful investigation before rushing into pitch mode.

If you're going to pitch a song to a particular artist, not only must the song/script be in keeping with the artist's image, but also a few music business executives must be persuaded to gamble a million dollars on it. A million? you ask me? Yes, a million!

Figure in the cost of sessions (studio, production, musicians, etc.), the video, tour support, radio school, stylists, and, of course, radio, and you are at a million big ones.

Your script - the script on which your song is built - has to function on a lot more levels than just entertaining your friends and family.

The Story and the Artist

What is the song about? Will this artist's audience identify him or her with this situation or circumstance? Does the artist use this language? Remember the only things that vary from genre to genre, aside from attitude, are vocabulary and technology. Vocabulary, especially, is a bond between the artist and the audience. That, by the way, is a huge obstacle from writers crossing over to cultures and genres with which they are not intimately connected or that they do not understand on a personal level.

Remember - It's About the Woman - *All* of Them

The song that you're going to write and pitch is a script for a performer. This as-yet-unnamed performer will then stand on stage and engage in a linear lyrical conversation with his or her audience (mostly women!)

We talked about this before. I'm going to talk about it again here, and I might talk about it again later, too. You're gonna get it. It's *all* about the women.

With rare exceptions, for stand-alone songwriters who plan on having a hit song, the paradigm to follow is this: men sing hit songs to women and women sing hit songs to women.

So, the mantra for the stand-alone songwriter parallels that of the restaurateur. When looking for a restaurant to invest in, there are three identical factors to consider: Location, location, location.

Likewise, to be a hit songwriter and write hit songs, there are three things to consider:

What's in it for the woman?

What's in it for the woman?

What's in it for the woman?

Remember, when you see the word "listener," mentally substitute the word "woman."

So, let's focus on the women's perception of your song.

Aside from the work being right for the artist's image and script, how can you tell if is it a potential hit?

Fish - Bait - Lure - Quick

Do you get the listener involved in the song quickly? (60 seconds including introduction.) I call it getting the listener to invest in your song. If I am going to be drawn into a songwriter's creation, I must identify with (or ideally become) the hero, victim, winner or loser in the piece.

Create and Fulfill Expectations - Surprise Me - Make It Interesting

Remember, you must create an expectation and then fulfill that expectation. Pull out some of your favorite songs and look at the titles/hooks – pretty average stuff, mostly words or phrases you use every day. However, those titles are the fulfillment of the created expectation.

The genius is in the creation of the expectation. Making something commonplace into something eye-catching – or in the case of the song, ear-catching – is your job.

If you have ever seen an uncut diamond, you know that they look remarkably unremarkable, rather boring, in fact. Only in the hands of someone who has absorbed the craft and mastered the skill of making the mundane sparkle will the seemingly dull come to life. The title is the destination, but the journey is the important part.

So, surprise me with interesting information, by asking a question with a different twist or by describing a condition, place, person or circumstance using words and phrases that make the ordinary extraordinary.

Singability is a Hidden Asset

As you're working your song according to the script you've devised for a specific artist, make sure that everything about the singability of the song is accessible: syllables, phrasing, range.

How easy is the song to sing? Are you trying to fit three-syllable words into a one-syllable spot? Remember that every song you grew up singing was easy to sing. The songwriters of those songs crafted them so that they were accessible for you.

The easy way to check the accessibility of your lyrics is to set up the recording device of your choice, set a metronome to the tempo you envision for your song and speak it into the recorder. Listen back. Wherever the words don't fit when you speak them, they won't fit when you sing them.

Oh, singer/songwriters do it all the time and get away with it because they are the artists. Stand-alone writers cannot get away with it.

Next, does your song's range span three notes or three octaves? Remember that a lot of "artistes" may have an abundance of charisma, personality and sex appeal but honestly can't sing very well. Send them the story songs, because the more detailed the story, the less melody you need.

The human animal is not very good at hearing more than one moving part at a time, and given a preference, will always defer to melody. That will distract them from the story and you don't want that! Remain linear when you tell your story.

To again quote my friend, Harlan Howard, "You don't change your chord 'til you change your thought!"

Rap - A Diversion

As I watched the rise of Rap some years ago, I loved it, but I was struck by its total lack of melody. What attracted the listener was the rhyme, the attitude, the revolutionary creative vocabulary, and the rhythm/beat. Of course, mindful of my mentors, I knew that, after the initial rush wore off, the writers would have to figure out a way to incorporate melody into the records. Knowing what a distraction melody can be from the lyrical content, it was driving me crazy to see at what point, and how, the writers would broaden their market and give the listeners more of what they needed so that the writers would enjoy long-term creative success.

In 1989, Biz Markie's *Just a Friend* featured Biz singing on the chorus, although I believe that track was more a symbolic refutation of the need for melody in Rap vocals. However, over 10 years later, when Nelly released his album, *Country Grammar*, there was a distinct sense of melody to his lyrical delivery. The songs felt like nursery rhymes, albeit nursery rhymes with some distinctly un-childlike themes, but there was enough melody to maintain the listener's interest.

Writing for the Big Voices

If you're pitching to divas or vocally well-endowed males, then be big on melody, heavy on monosyllabic words, heavy also on open vowel sounds (A-E-I-O-U-Y!), and minimal with story because the listener will be focused on the melody.

Did You Do The Job?

And finally, have you told the whole story – beginning, middle and end?

Have you created an expectation from the opening line, fulfilled that expectation in 60 seconds, added information/detail in the next verse, and spiced it up by adding conflict or calming it down? Have you made the listener laugh, cry, question, cheer, feel any (or all) of a whole range of emotions or just plain old fall in love?

Yes? Then job well done!

NOTES:

CHAPTER 15

WATCH OUT FOR LAND MINES

BY NOW, SOME OF THIS IS GOING TO FEEL REPETITIVE, but there's a reason for it. Just as your title needs to be repeated in a song for listeners to "get it," key points need to be reinforced. So, here are a dozen land mines that show up time and time again when I'm reviewing songs. These'll blow your song out of the water in an instant, honest!

1. Too much melody / Too little melody
2. Words that don't fit - inaccessible
3. Contrived rhymes
4. Changing rhyme scheme from verse to verse
5. An unexplained item
6. Changing pronouns
7. Too many ideas (2 songs glued together)

8. Not fulfilling an expectation

9. Mixing forms

10. Not changing rhyme scheme for the chorus

11. Repetitive words

12. Failing to satisfy the listener?

I am working on the assumption (there it is again, "writers assumption") that you have been writing for a while and will already know what I am talking about and will use this as a checklist rather than as a first time encounter with reality.

1. TOO MUCH MELODY/TOO LITTLE MELODY

Remember that what invites the listener in 100 percent of the time is melody. What keeps them there is lyric. If you're dealing with a story song, limit the melody to the actual hook where there is not a lot of story going on, or if you have a complex melodic structure, you will want to limit the amount of information you are trying to convey.

2. WORDS THAT DON'T FIT - INACCESSIBLE

You singer/songwriters are especially fond of doing this. You jam a three-syllable word into a two-syllable spot or a two-syllable word into a monosyllabic niche. Don't.

Remember being excluded at the party!
There is a hard and fast rule called the "Rule
of Accessibility." Simply stated, the "Rule of
Accessibility" is best explained by recalling every
song that has become a permanent part of your
musical landscape.

Easy to sing, weren't they?

The writer invited you in by making sure there
were no "speed bumps" to challenge you. There
are a couple of great ways to make sure there are
no "speed bumps" or "lumpy words."

You must be doing the inviting. The easiest way
is check for "speed bumps" or "lumpy words" is
to get a metronome and set it for the tempo that
you feel is appropriate for the song. Get your lyrics, turn on your recording device and speak the
lyric to the tempo.

Listen back.

Wherever a word doesn't fit when you speak it, it
will not fit when you sing it.

Oh, you can make it fit, but really it doesn't.
The distracted, drive-time listener will stumble
over this "speed bump" and be excluded. When
you exclude them and make it hard for them to

sing your song, they will simply reach for that radio and exclude you.

Bye, bye record.

Another way to evaluate the "singability" of your song is to get someone really good to sing it for you.

In my life I have tried to *never* sing my own demos. Starting out as a singer/songwriter, I have been fortunate enough to have had several record deals, but in the main. I have avoided singing my own "stand-alone" pitchable material. Try to find a great singer to perform your demos. It will give you a perspective on the song.

The best of these demo singers are future stars, and I have been fortunate to have used a lot of them over the years.

What you have to do is pay attention in the studio. Set the key that works for the singer, make sure the tempo is right, and then get out of the way and listen.

As they sing your song during the first couple of run-throughs, if there is a spot where they struggle to interpret your lyric, take that lyric sheet and rewrite on the spot.

If this "future star" can't sing your song easily at three in the afternoon, then what chance does the heavily-distracted listener have to sing along at 7:00 AM?

Again, I repeat, by making the listener work to sing your song you are making the listener feel excluded.

And you know how they will respond – by excluding you.

3. CONTRIVED RHYMES

Poetry and lyrics are almost always mutually exclusive. They have nothing to do with each other.

You use the devices of poetry (alliteration, metaphor, etc.) in a linear lyrical conversation.

Yes, a great lyric is a linear lyrical conversation between two people.

If you are trying to convince someone of the reality of your love for them and you say, "I love you, do you love me too, I think that we can make it through," chances are that they will think you're an idiot.

However, if you say, "I love you, I need you, I've got to be with you," you'll stand a better chance of winning their heart.

The former is a poem, the latter a lyric. The more conversational the lyric, the more enduring the hit.

There are several areas where predictability of the rhyme scheme is very important. Let's say you want to write church music or tavern, pub, or coffee house anthems. For those uses, the predictability of the rhyme scheme is telegraphed to the listener so that they can more easily join in. They are "invited in" by you setting up a rhyme scheme that they can anticipate and participate in quickly.

You've probably heard, in the course of your writing career, about hard rhymes vs. soft rhymes. Hard rhymes fit perfectly like "met" and "yet," "me" and "be," "life" and "wife." Soft rhymes are less perfect fits such as "pasture" and "matter" or "clever" and "together." One of the most notable soft rhymes was in the song. *Wind Beneath My Wings* where the writers, Jeff Silbar and Larry Henley, actually managed to make "hero" and "eagle" work.

Many years ago, writers were judged by the quality of their rhyme scheme. Hard rhyme was king. Even today, there are many successful writers who will agonize over a rhyme until they find the perfect word to make the hard rhyme.

We see soft rhymes used a lot in Pop and even more in Country. They seem to contribute to the conversationality of the songs. Hard rhymes are more prevalent in musical theater, nearly demanded, actually.

4. CHANGING RHYME SCHEME

While we are dealing in rhyme schemes, let me reinforce the obvious.

The rhyme scheme remains the same from verse to verse.

Having said that, you will probably hear songs on the radio that do not abide by this rule. Keep in mind that the artist or producer was probably the writer of the song. However, by varying the rhyme scheme from verse to verse they limit the potential of the song to be covered in the future and make it more difficult for the listener to sing along with the song, which is the ultimate goal.

Once you have established the pattern, the listener will have the expectation of being informed the same way from verse to verse.

However, having said that, you should change rhyme scheme verse to chorus. (See #10.)

The most recent time that I look at them, 100 percent of the #1 Billboard Pop and Country songs changed rhyme scheme from verse to chorus. Further, 9 of the 13 #1 Pop hits in 2009 did not rhyme the title/hook with any other lines within the body of the song. This technique makes the title/hook of the song stand out that much more.

Conversely, in Country it is far more likely that the title will rhyme with another line within the chorus. This may have something to do with Country music being more closely associated with Folk forms which often have a consistent rhyme scheme throughout.

The reason for the pattern shift is to alert the listener that something different is coming their way.

So, if you have an AABB verse, make sure you have an ABCB/AAAB (or some other variation) chorus. In reality, you can do anything you want, but when you are luring reluctant ears into your invention, use all the skills you possess. Changing rhyme scheme from verse to wherever you are leading them (lift, pre-chorus, chorus, etc.) helps keep listeners on track. If they're on track, they'll be requesters and purchasers.

However, in a lot of hit records you will see the writer changing rhyme scheme from verse to verse and getting away with it. Generally, those songs will have been written by the artist and/or the producer and/or as many people as are necessary to make it a hit. Luckily for them, there are many elements that will save the song and make it a hit, e.g., the video, the image of the artist, various types of media tie-ins and loads of money spent on promotion.

5. AN UNEXPLAINED ITEM

An unexplained item is simply an important detail which you have inserted into a song that does not fit into the pattern or context of the story. I'll go back to the Chekhov example again. If you have one of your characters running around in your song with a loaded pistol, the listener is going to want to know why the character has a gun. Big details which you do not sufficiently explain will take the listener out of the moment, cause confusion, and make it less likely that they will be able to internalize the song.

6. CHANGING PRONOUNS

I'm sure that I don't have to tell you that while rhyme scheme changes are desirable from section to sections, (not from verse to verse) pronoun shifts are tough tricks. If you have been talking about you and me throughout a song you had better set me up for *"you,"* *"me"* and *"us"* to become *"she"* or *"he"* or *"they."*

The Lennon/McCartney team did it brilliantly in *She's Leaving Home.* In that song, the narrator shifts from an outside perspective to the perspective of the parents at the end of the song. No matter how you alert me to the shifting pronoun, remember that it is essential that: first, you tell me; then, you tell me that you told me; and then, you remind me that you told me. Having said all that, however, you will see a lot of Pop records changing pronouns from section to section because there will be a different character or characters singing that part, e.g., Jay Sean featuring L'il Wayne or Lady Gaga featuring Colby O'Donis.

7. TOO MANY IDEAS
   (GLUEING TWO SONGS TOGETHER)

Speaking of mixing things up, if people are having a hard time following along from verse to chorus, there is always the chance that you may have stapled two different songs together.

If your verse is about your neighbor's barking dog and your chorus is about Christmas in Cleveland, chances are the connection between the two is known only to you. Uh oh. This is a serious disconnect. Re-evaluate immediatelly. Ready, Aim, Miss!

8. NOT FULFILLING EXPECTATIONS

Many times already I have mentioned that when you set the stage in your song, you will create expectations for the listener that something in particular is going to happen. If you do not fulfill those expectations, you will have disappointed your listener. Obviously, you can use those expectations to good effect to surprise the listener with a twist in the narrative of the song; but, somehow, some way, you will need to provide the listener with some sort of resolution.

9. REPETITIVE WORDS

If you say, "I saw the picture of a dog in your hand, and then I took a picture of you for my wallet. But you showed a picture of me to that other guy," the listener is going to get burned out on the repetition of the word, "picture."

Use synonyms. Buy a thesaurus. Even the word

"love," as wonderful as it is, can be worn out by relentless repetition.

10. NOT CHANGING RHYME SCHEME FOR THE CHORUS

If you decide not to change the rhyme scheme from the verse to chorus it is most likely that you are writing more in a folk style or in some genre where you have to invite the listener in very, very quickly. In certain genres, your goal is to get your audience to sing along with you, and by keeping the rhyme scheme consistent you make it easier to anticipate where the song is going. This works best for songs you'll be selling at 10 o'clock at night in the club or for anthems that you want to get people involved in quickly such as fight songs for sports teams or church music.

11. MIXING FORMS

Wandering from one form to another within the body of the story should be avoided. For instance, if you are working in Fifth Form (AABA) you will create problems for your listener if you turn the B section into a real chorus, and then add a bridge or middle eight.

Having created the expectation in the listener that you will have led them chronologically through the story by the end of the third A section, the listener's confusion becomes your problem when you carry them off to somewhere unexpected.

Remember, you as a movie-goer expect to be led through a film in a certain way. A listener (a linear woman) expects no less from your song. Having said all that, however, despite the fact that a highly-distracted listener is harder to manipulate, if the song feels good to you, go ahead a write it that way. It just may be a most wonderful 10 o'clock at night song.

A good illustration of how the mixing of forms can work is Owl City's *Fireflies* which blends Third and Fifth Forms.

12. FAILING TO SATISFY THE LISTENER?

Have you told the whole story? All the right details and no distracting ones? Will the listener want to hear it again? Is it easy to sing? Does it invite the listener in because it is about the listener or a situation the listener personally identifies with? If you have accomplished all of the above, you'll have a song that will make an excellent vehicle for an artist to communicate with their listeners.

NOTES:

CHAPTER 16

WRITE A HIT!
GET IT OUT THERE!

OKAY, SO WE'VE BEEN OVER THE BASICS, we've explored many aspects of craft, I've pointed out the pitfalls and land mines, and now it's time for you to get busy. One more ramble from me about process, and then it's time to hold your song up against the Murphy Song Checklist and get it out there.

Craft is Crucial!

In a hit song – and I stress *song* – not necessarily a vehicle for a hit record that requires massive production values and engineering skills, craft is a key factor. I am constantly told by big hit writers that they never read books on songwriting or that the Beatles never took a class.

What people seem to forget about the Beatles is that for years they did 40-minute shows four or five nights a week playing "cover" tunes ... songs that had been hits by other artists that their audiences loved and wanted to hear them sing. They got a sense of where to rhyme, where not to rhyme, where to place the "hook," and basic song structure. When confronted with the prospect of writing their own material, they had all the basics of hit songs ground into them. They were hardwired into the formula. All they had to do was put in their own attitudes, vocabulary and technology around traditional craft.

My friends who have managed to write hit songs also loved music as they were growing up. They found structures and craft that appealed to them, and imitated it, putting their own individual stamp on it.

In today's environment that scenario is rare. Since the '70s, DJs have dominated live music venues. How often do you see young cover bands playing multiple sets every night? Creators are given easy access to state-of-the-art equipment and left to their own devices. Most of what I hear is wonderfully produced, innovative, creative - and poorly crafted.

Create and Fulfill Expectation

You lure the listener to the "hook/nut."

How do you lure them?

What you do is create an expectation and then fulfill it.

Again, to paraphrase Chekov, if you introduce a loaded gun in the first act you had better fire it before the end of the play. You need to create an expectation in the audience that something dramatic is going to happen, and, by God, something dramatic better happen.

So, how do you accomplish the above?

Ask a Question. Why? Who? What? When? Then Answer it!

By beginning the song with an interrogative you are automatically engaging the listener, because, in their mind, they will want to know how you, as the songwriter, are going to answer the question.

If you look at *My Life Would Suck Without You*, performed by Kelly Clarkson, she asks the question "guess this means you're sorry?" She then explains what her significant other should be sorry for. In *River of Love*, performed by George Strait, he says "hey baby, won't you take a little ride with me," and then delivers you to "the river of love." In Jason

Aldean's *She's Country,* he poses the question "you boys ever met a real country girl," and then goes on to define what a "real" country girl actually is. Jason Derulo starts his song, *Whatcha Say,* with the question "what did she say?" He then goes on to answer that question.

Make a statement. Then illustrate it.

Beginning the song with a definitive declaration that piques the listener's attention will invite them to hang in there for the full 60 seconds that it will take for you to reach the hook. By stating that something is going to happen or that a fact or set of facts are true, you challenge the listener to engage with the story and stick around until the hook.

The Black Eyed Peas begin their song, *I Gotta Feelin,'* with the line "I gotta feelin' that tonight's gonna be a good night," and then spend the rest of the song detailing the different ways that they are going to get their party on. In Eminem's, *Crack a Bottle,* he states that now is the "the moment you've all been waiting for," and then introduces himself, Dr. Dre and 50 Cent, before detailing their collective adventures in the body of the lyrics.

Start with the opposite of the title.

For example, in *I Run To You,* performed by Lady Antebellum, the first three lines run counter to the sentiment of the title. They begin by saying "I run from hate, I run from prejudice, I run from pessimists," thereby creating contrast which may surprise the listener and make them want to know what the protagonist actually runs towards.

A Country radio listener may anticipate that a song entitled, *Small Town USA,* would be a tribute to small town American virtues, however, Justin Moore begins his song of the same title by stating that "a lot of people called it prison when I was growin' up." He resolves the song singing the praises of his upbringing in a small town, but by creating contrast with his first line he ensures that the listener will take that ride with him back to his roots.

The task is to create an expectation and then fulfill it. Put in a loaded gun to get the listener's attention and then make sure you fire the damn thing.

Above all, avoid unexplained details.

Again, this situation is your invention. Invite me in, don't leave it up to my imagination, pretend I don't have one.

Now what?

Your song is finished. You were eloquent. The melody flowed. You are fulfilled, complete. You resound with satisfaction. You said everything you wanted to say.

How could anyone fail to rush to record your song? Well, not so fast … Your songs may be your little lambs, but when it comes time to send one of them to the market, keep in mind that some people hate lamb chops and others are allergic to wool.

So before you proceed, think back … back to before you entered the music business; back to when you were the audience and went to see singers for fun; back to when you thought those singers were singing songs they had written about their own lives; back to when you thought you were catching a glimpse of their inner souls. You were unaware that those inner souls had been crafted for them by Bacharach & David or Holland-Dozier-Holland.

Well, just as most of your favorite TV and movie stars do not write their own scripts, luckily for songwriters, neither do a lot of singers write their own songs. That's changing rapidly in today's artist/producer/ publisher coalitions, but the chance still exists for a stand-alone writer with truly outstanding songs to get a cut that then becomes a hit.

Remember, the major difference between actors and singers is that while most actors can change characters from film to film, successful singers in today's image-driven market rarely depart radically from the persona (and sometimes their management) that they have chosen. The tabloids can always be counted on to exploit any of those deviations.

Careful pronoun perspective is the only way that you can write a song on a difficult subject, or about a villain, that a squeaky-clean performer can then propel into a hit. Pronouns are your friends.

In order to lure me/the listener in, it is better that you speak directly *to* me, not *about* me, don't go around in circles. Though I dealt with the pronoun (the little big word) in a previous chapter, let me remind you that when it comes to the song as a script, it is the little **huge** word.

Repeating: You'll get my attention faster if the song is about *You, I, Us* or *We,* because if it's about *Her, Him* or *Them,* it will be much harder to capture and keep my interest. Also, if the song is using the first-person pronoun (*you, me, I,* etc.) and the central figure is too old, too young, not hip, too angry, or just not the image that the artist, management or label wish to project, you might consider changing to the third-person pronoun (even though the odds are higher for your song not being #1).

When you make that change to third person, the artist can sing the song (about being homeless, a killer, or a drunk perhaps) without it reflecting personally on him or her.

Your song is a script for a performer to stand on stage and have a direct conversation with his or her audience. (In the case that I make convincingly, according to all the analysis and statistics, that audience is women! I told you I'd hammer this into you.)

In my opinion, if you are a stand-alone writer – not a performer, not in a band – and you are not writing for women, you are decreasing your chances for success! Our world of entertainment is always ultimately about "The Woman." With rare exceptions, it is men singing to women and women singing to women.

So, the mantra for the songwriter parallels that of the retail store (or the restaurant we talked about in Chapter 14). When looking to open a retail store, there are three factors to consider: location, location, location. Likewise, to be a songwriter, there are three people you should consider: the woman! the next woman! one more woman!

So, when you see the word LISTENER in any advice about songwriting from anyone, not just me, mentally substitute the word WOMAN. You do get it by now, right?

So let's focus on their perception of your song. These are the ways to reach women listeners, trust me.

Do you get the listener involved in the song quickly? How quickly?

Well, all of my research bears out that 60 seconds, including introduction, is your maximum window. I call it getting the listener to invest in your song. If I am drawn into a writer's invention, it requires me to identify with (or ideally become) the hero, victim, winner or loser in the piece.

Next, you must create an expectation and then fulfill that expectation. Pull out some of your favorite songs and look at the titles – pretty average stuff, mostly words or phrases you use every day. However, those titles are the fulfillment of the created expectation. The genius is in the creation of the expectation. Making something commonplace eye-catching – or in the case of the song, ear catching – is your job.

Well, I guess we need to have a checklist for this song that you have chosen to be a script for a specific artist. We'll get there in the next chapter, but here's a sneak preview/review.

High on that checklist is accessibility.

How easy is the song to sing?

Are you trying to fit three-syllable words into a one-syllable spot?

Does its range span three notes or three octaves?

What is the song about?

Will this artist's audience identify him or her with this situation or circumstance? Remember all that changes from genre to genre, aside from attitude, is vocabulary and technology.

Vocabulary, especially, is a bond between the artist and the audience. That, by the way, is a huge obstacle for writers crossing to cultures and genres that they are not intimately connected to or understand personally.

Are all parts of the story included? Nothing left out? Have you created some tension from the opening line?

Have you reached the crux of the story in 60 seconds, added information and detail as you moved through the form, and ramped up the interest by adding some conflict or smoothing things out?

Have you reached the listener emotionally? When you play your song out do people laugh, tear up, feel angry, cheer joyfully, smile broadly, clap along, sway in their seats, or just plain old fall in love?

They do?

Then take it to the artist – way to go! But, get it professionally demo'd first.

Why Not Sing Your Own Demos

After performing at a songwriters' showcase once, an A&R person I'd known for years asked me why – as I obviously sang reasonably well – she had never heard my voice on any of the song demos I'd pitched to her. Here are the four reasons I gave – think about them as they relate to you - are you an artist or a stand-alone writer?

1. Confusion

The question will be asked: "Are you looking for an artist deal, or is this just to pitch the artist on the roster?" Bearing in mind that the function of an A&R person is to reject the bulk of what he or she hears, chances are if they don't like your voice, your song might go down with you.

2. Association

Back in the early 1980s, Garth Brooks, T. Graham Brown, Kathy Mattea, and many more all sang song demos when they first came to town. If they had sung one of your songs when they were starting out, your work and name just might have rung a bell when you submitted them a song later on their careers. Or, they might remember singing a demo on a song that went nowhere, but that resonated with them. The more people in the song's circle, the more likely it will find a home.

Really great singers still do demos today, hoping to get picked up for a deal. When you are competing with every writer on the planet for attention from a major artist, every edge helps. Relationships are priceless, cultivate them.

3. Last-Chance Insurance To Get It Right

Once you are in the studio and the track is going down, listen to how easily the singer locks into the lyric. If at any point, he or she stumbles even slightly on a word or a phrase – re-write immediately. The word "irreconcilable" may be a wonderful word, but there's probably a better way to say "it's over." Remember, if the hot demo singer you are using has a problem with the lyric, so will the artist you are aiming the song at.

4. Personal Preference

Most people hate the sound of their own voice.

<u>NOTES:</u>

<u>**CHAPTER 17**</u>

THE MURPHY SONG CHECKLIST

USE THE FOLLOWING checklist to make sure that you've covered all the bases after you create your song.

1. 60 seconds to first use of title

2. Did you explain the premise of the song?

3. Did you establish the structure of the song?

4. Did you invite the listener in?

5. What would a distracted woman at the worst time of day think of the character of the singer?

6. Is the singer's role as it is portrayed in the song consistent with the persona of the artist you will pitch it to (age, do they have children, employment)?

7. Is the story set up with ear catching new detail?

8. Is the hook/title properly set up (and, if, but) make a statement, ask a question, etc.?

9. Is the hook/title memorable because it was properly set up and the melody complements it?

10. Is the language consistent with character and setting?

Then, answer these questions:

Have you kept your pronouns consistent? If it's *"she"* in the verse, it should not be *"you"* in the chorus (unless you left *"she"* for *"you"*).

Have you varied your rhyme scheme from the verse to the chorus to subtly alert the listeners that something (the hook) is coming their way?

Is there a significant change in the melody from the verse to the chorus?

Do the opening couple of lines of the first verse set the stage for the story that follows?

Is the hook in the right place? With rare exceptions, the title/hook is placed at the end of the chorus, not somewhere in the verse or the backyard.

Is the language you use to tell your story contemporary, would you hear it in normal day-to-day conversation?

FINALLY, I LEAVE YOU WITH WHAT I CONSIDER THE MOST IMPORTANT POINTS:

Is the song satisfying?

Does it have a beginning, a middle, and an end?

If the answer to all of the above is yes, demo on!

NOTES:

CHAPTER 18

BRIEF OVERVIEW OF COPYRIGHT

I'M GOING TO SPEND A FEW PAGES talking about the copyright side of music. I want you to get a sense of how your songs are going to be protected. You've put too much work into them to neglect this important task.

I have asked my son, Shawn Murphy, who teaches at Columbia College in Chicago, to give a brief overview of copyright.

Understanding copyright:
The system of copyright protection which we have in the United States is fairly user-friendly and provides protection at the federal level for your intellectual property. There are a few things that you should be aware of, though:

1. You MUST register your songs with the Library of Congress (LOC) in order to bring a suit in federal court. Although your songs are considered to be your intellectual property as soon as they are "fixed in a tangible medium of expression," you cannot sue for damages, or even prevent an infringement from continuing, without filing a registration with the LOC. Simply go to www.copyright.gov and fill out an ECO form.

2. There are two types of copyrights you can file pertaining to music. The first is for the "underlying composition." This is essentially the sheet music for the song. This abstract, pre-recording, idea of the song is copyrightable by itself. You should definitely file any compositions that you plan on publishing with the LOC.

   Many, or even most, writers do not chart their song out on sheet music as they are creating it. Because it's so cheap and easy to make a recording of your song, you will probably record the song as you are writing it. Just remember that each recording that you make qualifies for its own copyright. If you ever plan to publish those early demos you will want to file separate copyrights for them with the LOC.

3. The duration of copyright will be for your lifetime plus 70 years. In the case of a song written by multiple writers, the 70 years doesn't begin until the year that the last surviving co-writer passes away. This is obviously a long time, but it actually works in favor of making more content available to the public. Why would a songwriter's heirs go to the trouble of producing technologically modern recordings of songs which have passed into their control unless there is a way for them to get back some of the money that they have to invest in creating those recordings? There is a vast amount of work (songs, photographs, etc.) which have passed into what is referred to as the public domain. That means that they are the common property of all of us, and we can do whatever we want with them without having to compensate the original creators. However, it is difficult to find many of those works because there are no caretakers for them anymore.

If the economic value of a song is zero, our society relies on libraries and museums to maintain that legacy for us. With so many people constantly creating in this country, you have to imagine that it's a very small percentage of those creations that survive from generation to generation. A longer duration of copyright incentivizes a songwriter's heirs to keep track of, and potentially to continue to make available, older works to the public.

4. Be mindful of the fact that you have a right of "first use." This means that you, as the writer of the song, have the exclusive right to determine who makes the first publicly issued recording of that song.

   However, once the song has been recorded and released, any other artist can make and release their own recording of your song. You cannot stop them! The new artist (in order to record the song) will get a mechanical license from the Harry Fox Agency and pay you 9.1 cents for each copy they manufacture or sell as a download.

   If you are writing a song for a particular artist, you will want to make sure that you do not make it available for download anywhere prior to that artist recording the song! A single download can be considered "distributing copies." That means that you have blown your right of first use, and the song is fair game for any artist.

   Record companies spend lots of money to promote an artist's single, and they typically don't want to have to deal with multiple versions of that song being recorded by other artists, not

even the writer(s). Always remember that we are
in the music business. The moment you create
a song you become one of the world's small
"businesses."

Learn how to protect it.

NOTES:

<u>CHAPTER 19</u>

MAKING THE MOST OF YOUR SONGWRITING SEMINAR

The next time you attend a songwriting seminar, take advantage of some of the tips that I've discovered – and a few pet peeves I've encountered – along the way.

1. **Arrive fully prepared.**

   Be ready to take notes. If you're using a laptop/ iPad make sure that it's fully charged or there are electrical outlets at hand. Remember that with electronic stuff it has a tendency to need to "wake up", so strangely enough old-fashioned works well. The best idea is to buy a small, lined notebook that does not have removable pages. Also bring two pens or two pencils...or both. (The other Murphy's Law will prevail and at least one of the two won't work). If you want to record the critique of your song, make sure you ask whether recording is permitted. One thing I have noticed is that panelists are a little less forthcoming when they know that they are being recorded! If you want the information "warts and all", at the very least, don't record the whole seminar, just your critique.

2. **Be sociable.**

   It's important to get to know your fellow partici-pants. There is usually time for coffee and con-versation before or after the sessions and during breaks. Remember, these songwriters are your peer group; networking and making contacts with them is essential. Professionals make it part of their lives, you should, too.

3. **Hold that thought during panels.**

   You will have at least one burning question rang-ing from contracts to demo quality. Don't ask until some part of the seminar touches on it. Throwing in a question on publishing when the panelists' focus is on song crafting will break the momentum and flow that the panel is trying to establish. If your burning question has not been answered at the end of the session, there's usually a question and answer period provided for just that reason.

4. **Take your best shot.**

   Bring your most recent and best shot to the critique session. The mistakes you were making five years ago aren't as relevant as the ones you are making today. Also, if you had a chance to pitch a song to a major-label artist, I doubt that you would choose your second-best or third-best song, so why do so with other professionals? Most people should be fine with you recording your song critique but... always ask.

5. **Don't bail out early.**

Once your song has been critiqued, don't just get up and leave. Chances are pretty high that during the session, you will hear a variety of problems similar to the ones you've encountered in songs other than the one you had critiqued. Now is your chance to hear professionals address, and remedy, those mistakes.

6. **Be courteous to your critiquers.**

Once your song has been critiqued, do not give another one to the professionals involved with your group. They have given of their time and expertise to help you. For you to expect them to critique another song and correspond with you – especially after they've given up a day or weekend that they could have used for at least a dozen other projects – is unreasonable and impolite. Believe me, this is a definite "No-No."

7. **Follow-up.**

However, if someone approaches you and asks if you have more music, be prepared to send them something immediately. Follow-up is critical. Busy people have the attention span of a gnat.

8. **Use the resources they suggest.**

If a speaker or reviewer mentions a website or a magazine or a book, read it, check it out. There's a reason that they are directing you to more information. They truly want you to succeed, and have just handed you a tool.

NOTES:

CHAPTER 20

LOOKING BACK ON WHAT'S TO COME!

I'D LIKE TO HAVE A FEW FINAL WORDS with you about how to make your songs stronger in the long-term, rather than in the short-term.

Mentoring Full Circle

Like most writers starting out in the music business, I was fortunate to have been adopted by several fine veteran writers. Why they took the time to give me a few words of advice, a moment of praise, a hard jab of criticism, or a cold beer of consolation was always a mystery to me. I never quite understood when they told me that a songwriter's best friend was not an artist, a label, a publisher, or a radio or TV station, but another songwriter.

While I worked on my craft, demoed my songs, hunted for a publisher, relentlessly chased that first recording, and hungered for that first hit, those veteran writers were doing all that and more. They were also working tirelessly to protect their copyrights and receive fair compensation for their work. In so doing, they were also looking after my rights and the rights of all fledgling writers.

At a recent NSAI's Pro Division meeting, I was talking to some of my contemporaries when it hit me that we had become my early mentors; and the sheep had become the shepherds. Just as our mentors had carried on the fight for copyright protection, so have we been continuing that fight through NSAI, as well as through the Songwriters Guild of America, ASCAP, and other songwriter organizations.

The Next Generation

Now as we look forward to another year, remember that the technology coming down the pike will eclipse anything that we have experienced to date. The technology will have one function–to use, in as many ways as possible, the work that we have dedicated our lives to creating. And if the history has taught us anything, it is that since the 1908 Copyright Law was put into place, users of music have done everything in their power to avoid paying creators for their music.

That's why it's important for you as a songwriter and a creator of music to join in the battle for copyright protection … so that you will be prepared to take the torch and lead the next generation of creators forward in the age where technology will make it increasingly easier for others to rob us of our work.

It's Your Life and Livelihood

Remember your songs are yours for Lifetime Plus 70 years. So, long after you're gone – if you have done your job well – your great, great grandchild may be able to afford an operation, a car, or a college education, compliments of you. When you earn your first gold record, you'll find that it comes with something else – a sword and a shield.

Write on!

NOTES:

ACKNOWLEDGMENTS

FIRST OF ALL, many thanks to all the amazing writers who in my professional life have shown me how to be a professional. In the assembly of this book there have been so many who have suggested, nudged and helped. These are just a few.

~ Of course, my best friend Louise, for encouraging and tolerating me grumping my way through the last three years.
~ Mark Ford, Phil Goldberg, Gerilyn Pearse, Jessica Tompkins, Anna Maki, Bryce Mims, Kaitlin Thorne, Michael Laskow, and of course, the wonderful Barbara Thornton.
~ My friends Todd and Jeff Brabec, without whose constant nagging, the book would not have been attempted.
~ My son Shawn Murphy, who brought as much information and commitment to this book as he does when he teaches his college class. Your father and student thanks you.
~ Kerry Murphy, whose willingness to shape and poke and prod and drag this project from inception to the finish line made this book possible.
~ I appreciate the keen eye and organizational skills of my patient editor, Peggy Glenn, in helping to make this book better than it was the first time.
~ Finally, thank you Lynn Snyder for sprinkling magic dust on it to make it a cake… it's a book! Who knew!